RED B

Wide Range Readers

Phyllis Flowerdew

Oliver & Boyd

Illustrated by Tony Morris

OLIVER & BOYD
Pearson Education Limited
Edinburgh Gate
Harlow
Essex CM20 2JE
An Imprint of Longman Group UK Ltd

First published 1982
Sixteenth impression 2003

© Phyllis Flowerdew 1982
All rights reserved; no part of this publication may be reproduced, stored in a retrieval system, or transmitted in any form or by any means, electronic, mechanical, photocopying, recording, or otherwise without the prior written permission of the Publishers or a licence permitting restricted copying in the United Kingdom issued by the Copyright Licensing Agency Ltd, 90 Tottenham Court Road, London, W1P 0LP.

ISBN 0 05 003081 7

Printed in Singapore (FOP)
SK/11

The publisher's policy is to use paper manufactured from sustainable forests.

Preface

There are eight Wide Range Readers Red Books. Books 1–6 can be used alone or with Wide Range Readers Blue and Green, with which they are parallel, and Books 7 and 8 follow on from the Book 6 level. The controlled vocabulary of Books 1–6 makes them suitable for children with the following reading ages:

7 to $7\frac{1}{2}$ years	– Book 1
$7\frac{1}{2}$ to 8 years	– Book 2
8 to $8\frac{1}{2}$ years	– Book 3
$8\frac{1}{2}$ to 9 years	– Book 4
9 to 10 years	– Book 5
10 to 11 + years	– Book 6

Books 7 and 8 are necessarily more loosely controlled but are broadly suitable for reading ages 11 to 12 and 12 to 13. Their subject matter is parallel to the Book 6 level and Books 7 and 8 are therefore suitable for children needing further graded reading practice before transferring completely to independent reading.

Contents

Lone Wolf 5
The Enchanted Tower 18
The Singing Boy 28
Choice for Maria 37
The Boy Who Never Was 52
William the Guillemot 56
The Blizzard 66
The Story of Joseph 81
King of Jazz 99
Bits and Pieces 111
Fire and Ice 115
The Lost Woman of San Nicolas 133
Very Short Stories 142
Mad About Bones 146
Lion of Two Worlds 160
More Iguanodons 174

Lone Wolf

They called it a wild-life park but it was really just a small, private zoo on the edge of the town. It was beautifully kept and the animals were given as much space as possible, though the wolves were really the only ones to have anything approaching their natural habitat – a small conifer forest called the Wolf Wood. Martin took little notice of the wolves because they were usually at the far side of the wood, prowling or dozing in the shadows. Today, Friday, as he put down his money at the turnstile, the man who sold the tickets said to him,

"You here again? You come every Friday after school, don't you?"

"Just about," replied Martin gruffly, without a smile.

The man passed him the ticket and added,

"Pretty quiet at this time of year, isn't it?" Martin nodded, but would not be drawn into conversation beyond a muttered "thank you".

As he went through the turnstile and into the zoo, one of the keepers entered the ticket office.

"Strange boy that," he said to the ticket man.

"Yes. Always alone. Comes nearly every Friday. Never a smile out of him."

"Spends a lot of time with the birds lately," said the keeper. "Tries to imitate their cries when he thinks there's no one around. Sea lions too. I've heard him make a pretty good sea lion noise."

"Probably got some idea of becoming an animal impersonator – on the telly."

"Mm, strange boy."

Most people thought Martin was a strange boy. He walked quietly back and forth each day to school where he did not do particularly well. He never seemed to play with other children. He seemed to have no friends.

He was, in fact, not really strange. He was a quiet, shy boy, rather sad and anxious and tangled up inside. Perhaps it was because of his mother and father. They had not lived together for more than a year. Martin was fond of them both. He lived with his mother, but every two weeks, on Saturday morning, he went by bus to stay with his father till Sunday evening. Mother, father, mother, father. It was an unsatisfactory life. He never quite knew where he was. One good thing about his father was that he always gave him some money – rather too much for a boy of his age. He gave it to try and make up for the fact that he saw so little of his son. The money was useful. It paid for the zoo ticket every Friday.

Martin's mother worked at the check-out of a supermarket, and on Fridays the shop stayed open until half-past seven. It was no fun going home to an empty house so Martin usually went to the zoo for a while. He loved animals. He felt nearer to them than to humans. He had some idea of trying to learn their language. They seemed to like him. They didn't criticise him or think he was strange. They seemed more like friends.

It was early autumn now. The days were rather cold and the zoo closed at six o'clock. It was Friday again and Martin was walking along the usual route to the entrance. He passed two women gossiping outside a house. He felt them look at him and he noticed that they lowered their voices. All the same he heard what they said.

"Strange boy, that," remarked one of them.

"Yes. Bit of a lone wolf, isn't he?" Lone wolf!

Martin didn't feel upset or annoyed. He didn't mind being called a lone wolf. He didn't mind at all. It was rather nice.

That day he went straight to the Wolf Wood. He stood at the railings and began to study the wolves. He counted twelve of them, but there were two or three others out of sight. Those he could see were in a loose group, growling and yelping a little as if they were discussing something. They were long-bodied and grey with tails hanging straight down. Their ears were rigid and pointed and their eyes were slanting. Quietly, Martin tried to imitate the sounds they were making, the deep growls, the higher yelps, the occasional howl. Sometimes some of the wolves glanced across at him. They appeared to be listening to him. He felt pleased. Lone wolf. He was a lone wolf. He felt a bond between the wolves and himself.

At home, he practised wolf talk and he looked forward to Fridays with real pleasure. At the Wolf Wood he listened and imitated and watched. When the wolves howled he would answer. When they were silent he could soon rouse them with his own voice. He was delighted with his progress, but sometimes he felt it wise to act in a somewhat secretive way. One keeper in particular appeared to resent his gifts of imitation.

"Oh you again," he was inclined to say crossly.

"You move on. You're exciting them. Go and talk to the cockatoo."

One afternoon the wolves seemed particularly restless. They were at the far side of the wood and Martin could see several of them walking in single file behind the leader of the pack, in and out among the trees. Martin gave a low wail and the wolves answered. He raised his voice to a howl and they joined in. It sounded eerie, but Martin often thought it was a song, not a cry. He was sure the wolves enjoyed it.

"I wish you wouldn't do that," said someone behind him. It was the keeper again. "You're upsetting them." Martin knew he wasn't upsetting them. They were enjoying themselves. It was no good trying to explain this to the keeper, so he said nothing and the keeper thought he was a surly boy and made his usual remark about talking to the cockatoo.

Next morning at breakfast time Martin's mother had the radio switched on for the news. Martin came in just as it was over.

"Did you hear that?" asked his mother.

"No. What was it about?"

"The wild-life park. Six wolves have escaped. They tunnelled their way out under a fence in the night. People are warned to keep their pets indoors for safety until the wolves are caught."

"They'll have a job to catch them," said Martin.

"They'll use tranquilliser darts."

"I wonder how far the wolves got before the keepers missed them. Where do you think they'll go, Mum?"

"One of the woods I should think. There are plenty in this district, aren't there? Be careful when you go out."

"Wolves don't usually attack people unless they're desperately hungry – or afraid."

The news buzzed round the town all day. Rumours

buzzed round too, rumours that someone had seen them, rumours that they had killed cats, dogs, chickens; and frightened children and old ladies. None of this was true at all, for in fact no one caught a glimpse of the wolves from morning till night. They had had plenty of time to get well away before their absence had been discovered, and the district outside the town was extensively wooded. Police cars and zoo officials drove round and round and found not a trace of them – not a footprint, not a sign of any sort. On Saturday night they were still free.

On Sunday morning Martin walked to the zoo. He was glad this wasn't his father's weekend. He found a notice on the zoo gate, saying "Closed". There was a van outside just about to set off on another search. Two of the keepers were walking towards it. One of them was the man who sometimes grumbled at Martin. At any other time Martin would not have said a word, but he was so anxious to hear the news that he said eagerly,

"Have you caught any of the wolves?"

"No," was the reply. "We don't even know where they are yet."

Martin hesitated. Then he said,

"I could find them for you." He didn't say it boastfully. He said it quietly and confidently. One of the men gave an amused chuckle at the thought and they walked on towards the van. Then the one Martin called the "grumpy" one stepped back and said to him,

"How would you set about catching them, then?"

"I should drive to the woods and call them, and if there was no answer I'd drive on further and call again. Twilight would be the best time. *I'd* be able to tell you where they were. Really I would."

"I believe you would," said the keeper slowly. "Tell me your name and address and maybe I'll persuade the head-keeper to come and pick you up tonight."

"Martin Roberts," said Martin. "I live in Sloane Street – number five."

. . . . . .

That evening at dusk, Martin, to his great delight, was included in the zoo search party. There were two

vans and a police car; and the town veterinary surgeon was there as well as keepers and police and two strangers armed with guns and tranquilliser darts. The weather was cool and calm with scarcely a breath of wind. The vans drove beyond the first stretch of wood and along beside the one that was called "Dark Forest".

"Try here, shall we?" said the vet. He and the others stepped out with Martin and walked silently along the forest trail.

"Now," said the vet to Martin. Martin stood still and took a deep breath. He started very softly in a low, monotonous wail. Gradually he raised his voice to a high yelp, and then to a loud, long-drawn-out howl. It sounded uncanny. The men looked at each other, quiet and somewhat awed. They all listened intently and waited hopefully for an answer. There was none. There was not a sound, not a movement. There was not a crackling of a twig nor a sign of any life.

"Try again," whispered the vet. Martin tried again, and people who lived within range of his voice must certainly have thought they were hearing a wolf.

Back in the van, the men were full of praise and admiration for Martin.

"How *do* you do it?" they asked.

"I don't know," he replied. "I can do other animals too – and birds."

"He's good at the cockatoo," added the "grumpy" keeper with a friendly grin. "Where now?"

The next stop was at Western Woods, which joined on to Dark Forest and followed the line of the road for a very long way. Martin tried in two different places there, but without success. Then there was Fawke Forest. It was almost dark now.

"Good luck, Martin," said one of the marksmen, crossing his fingers. Martin stood between the trees in Fawke Forest and took a deep breath. Once more he started softly in a low, monotonous wail. Gradually he raised his voice to a high yelp, and then to a loud, long-drawn-out howl. It sounded uncanny. He took another breath and kept the sound going – the song of the wolves – a song, not a cry. Now, unbelievably, there was the sound of another voice joining in – and another and another. It was the wolves in chorus, answering, echoing through the trees, somewhere in Fawke Forest.

The men looked at each other. Now they knew where the wolves were. All they had to do was to advance and close in and fire their darts and carry the unconscious animals to the vans. Martin felt a little unhappy about this. It seemed unnecessary and undignified.

"Can't I try to get them round to the van?" he asked softly. "I'm sure I could do it, if you would let me go to them."

"I dare say you could," said the vet, "but it's a risk we daren't let you take. Just do the call again so that we can begin to close in and let the marksmen get nearer."

On Monday morning it was in the daily papers, "Wolves all captured. Boy calls wolves." The story was told in different ways in different papers, but all had Martin's name in print.

At school everyone flocked round him.

"Was it you, Martin? Was it really you?"

"How did you do it? How did the police know you could do it?"

"What happened? Tell us the whole story."

"Make a wolf call now. Go on. Do it here."

During the morning a newspaper photographer called and took a photograph of Martin in the classroom with a number of children grouped round him. They were all delighted at the publicity.

"I believe you're a bit of a lone wolf yourself, Martin, aren't you?" said the photographer.

"Oh no," replied a boy called Tim. He had scarcely ever taken notice of Martin before, but now he spoke with pride and affection. "He's not a lone wolf. He's one of the pack."

And that wasn't the end of the story. The owner of the zoo presented Martin with a digital wrist watch and a special ticket that would admit himself and a friend to the wild-life park as often as he wished, for the rest of his life. Something else happened too. The next evening he took his mother to the zoo; and at the same time his father went to see the wolves. They all met unexpectedly outside the Wolf Wood and stared a little awkwardly at each other and the wolves. They were beautiful animals, long-bodied and grey, with tails hanging straight down. Their ears were rigid and pointed and their eyes were slanting. Very strongly, Martin felt the bond between the wolves and himself. Now, he felt too, for the first time in his life, that there was a bond between his classmates and himself. He was no longer a lone wolf. He was one of the pack.

Now his mother was talking to his father.

"Come home and have a cup of tea with us," she said.

The Enchanted Tower

There is an old Spanish story that tells of a great tower said to have been built by Hercules himself, near the ancient city of Toledo. Little was known about it except that it was kept locked and guarded through the centuries. It was said that no one had ever entered it and come out alive. The ordinary people made no attempt to solve its mystery, but King Roderick was curious about it. It was within his kingdom. Why was it always locked? He was the king. Why should he not enter it? These thoughts came to him from time to time and he was most interested, therefore, when two old men begged an audience with him, to speak to him of the mystery of the tower.

He sat upon his throne and received them. They were dressed in long white robes fastened with girdles bearing the signs of the zodiac, and hung about with many keys, keys of iron and steel and silver, and keys that were so old that they were coated in rust. The two old men bowed low and said,

"Hear us, O King. You know that Hercules built a strong tower near this ancient city of Toledo. Within it he left a magic spell. At the entrance he erected a great gate of iron, fastened with locks of steel. He decreed that each new king of Spain should add a new lock to the gate and he prophesied woe and destruction to anyone who should open it. Through the centuries the gate has been guarded, from the days of Hercules until this very hour. No one has ever passed into the tower. Now, O King, we have come to ask you to put your own lock upon the gate, as all the kings before you have done."

King Roderick was silent for a moment. Then he said,

"I will do this, but first tell me the mystery of the tower."

"That we cannot do," replied the aged men, "but ancient records declare the gate will be opened only by a king who will be the last of his line, at a time when his empire will be tottering." So saying, the old men bowed low and departed.

Roderick was left more curious than ever. What was there inside the tower? Why should he not enter it and look?

"I will put a new lock upon the gate," he told his counsellors, "but first I will open it and solve the mystery."

"But the old men foretold woe and destruction," warned the counsellors. "They spoke of a king whose empire will be tottering."

"Spain is not tottering," argued Roderick, "and there should be no secrets kept from its king. I tell you, I will go to the tower and open the gate."

In spite of all protests and all warnings, Roderick rode forth a few days later, in company with a small band of his knights and soldiers. The tower stood on a high rock surrounded by even higher cliffs and deep precipices. Roderick had never ridden so close to it before and he saw that its walls were built of marble and green jasper, inlaid with precious jewels that caught the sun and flashed and sparkled in its rays. An entrance-passage had been cut through the rock and at the end of it was the great iron gate, bolted and barred and fastened with the locks of all the kings of Spain from the time of Hercules.

Standing one on each side of the gate were the two old men who had visited the king in Toledo. When they saw him approaching with his followers they thought he had come to put his own lock upon the gate and they bowed low and stood aside for him.

"I ask you to open the gate for me," said Roderick.

"But evil will come of it, O King!" protested the old men in horror.

"I command you to open the gate for me," said Roderick. He was king. He had to be obeyed. Fumbling and frightened, and foretelling ill, the old men fitted the keys into the rusty locks. Each key seemed more difficult to turn than the one before it. The king, knights and soldiers helped, struggling to undo the locks of centuries, one after the other, one after the other. It was morning when the king's party had arrived at the tower. It was nearly sundown when the last of the locks was undone and the gate swung open for Roderick, King of Spain.

The gate led into a hall, with a door on the further side guarded by a huge bronze figure of a man holding a mace. Roderick paused, for though the figure was of bronze it appeared to have life and strength.

"I command you to let me pass," said the king. "I will do no harm. I wish to learn the mystery of the tower." Slowly the great figure raised its mace above its head and allowed the king and his followers to pass beneath it, through the door and into a second hall. The walls of this hall glimmered with specks of gold and patterns of precious stones – emeralds and rubies, crystals and amethysts.

In the middle of the hall was a table, and on it was a casket with these words engraved upon it:

"In this casket is the mystery of the Tower. Only the hand of a king can open it, but let him beware, for events of the future will be shown to him."

The king hesitated and glanced at his followers.

"Events of the future. There can be no harm in that," he said. Slowly he pushed back the lid of the casket and everyone pressed forward to look inside.

The first feeling was of disappointment. There appeared to be nothing there except a large piece of parchment folded carefully between two plates of copper. The king nodded to two of his knights and they took out the parchment, unfolded it and spread it wide, holding it up for all to see. It was a picture of fierce-looking men on horseback. They were bearing bows and arrows and scimitars, the curved sharp blades of the east, and above them was written,

"Rash king, behold those who shall hurl thee from thy throne and subdue thy kingdom."

Roderick and his followers were silent, and as they gazed upon the picture the figures of the horsemen began to move. They began to hurl their lances and shoot their arrows, to swing their battle-axes and strike with their scimitars. With the vision came the sound of warfare, the clash of steel and the beating of drums, the shout of the victors and the cries of the wounded.

One of the armies was the army of Spain, bearing flags showing the cross of the Christians. The other army was of darker men from across the narrow strip of sea. They were beating the Spaniards, pressing them back and back and treading their falling banners in the mud.

As King Roderick watched in horror he saw a soldier wearing a crown and armour with his own colours and his own coat of arms. The soldier's back was towards him but he knew he was watching himself. He saw too that the warrior's white war-horse was his own beloved steed, Orelia. At that moment the soldier was felled to the ground and lost to sight and Orelia galloped wild and riderless through the battlefield.

Roderick and his followers dared watch no longer.

They turned and rushed out of the enchanted tower. The great bronze figure at the inner door had gone and the two aged gate-keepers lay dead at the entrance. Lightning slashed at the rocks outside and thunder roared and rumbled as the king and his men scrambled out in fear. There was a terrifying crack and the tower burst into flames, stones split and leaped with the heat, and swiftly the tower crumbled and collapsed into a pile of ashes that were blown and scattered far and wide by the winds of heaven.

. . . .

This much is all myth, but perhaps the story was invented to explain and excuse the events that followed, when Roderick was indeed hurled from his throne and his kingdom was subdued – subdued for nearly eight hundred years – from seven hundred and eleven to fourteen hundred and ninety two.

The truth is this:

While Roderick was King of Spain, the Moors in Africa were casting covetous eyes upon his kingdom, and in the year seven hundred and eleven a Moorish commander named Tarik landed with an army on the southern tip of Spain. This was the place now called Gibraltar (from Arabic words meaning "the mountains of Tarik"). Roderick was busy in the north of the country at the time, but when he heard the news he rode to Cordoba, summoned his army and advanced upon the Moors. It was an impressive sight – the king in shining armour, under a splendid canopy, at the head of thousands of soldiers. The Moors quailed at the sight but Tarik cried out,

"Men, the enemy is upon you and the sea is at your backs. Your only escape is in courage and valour!" At this rallying cry the men took fresh heart and shouted,

"We follow you, O Tarik!" Then all rushed into battle which continued for a week, with many reports of brave deeds on both sides. Roderick might eventually have won but treachery and desertion among his men turned fortune against him and his army was beaten and scattered. The Moors advanced, capturing Cordoba and Toledo; and soon all Spain was in their power.

Roderick meanwhile had vanished. His horse and his sandals were found on the bank of a river but he was not with them. Doubtless he had been wounded and killed by the enemy, or perhaps drowned and washed out to sea. For many years his people believed he was living on some distant island and that one day he would return, healed of his wounds, to lead the Christians again against the invader.

The Singing Boy

When King Charles the Second came riding into London town to ascend the throne in the year 1660, little Henry Purcell was just about one year old. Probably his father held him up to see the streets hung with flags and strewn with flowers, and no doubt he heard the ringing of the church bells, clanging and echoing to welcome the King. He would, of course, remember nothing of this, though it was going to make a great difference to his life, for Henry was destined to be a singing boy; and it was Charles the Second who brought back choirs and organs and anthems to the churches of England and gave boys like Henry a very important place in which to sing.

The King had been in exile for twelve years and

the country had been ruled by Oliver Cromwell and the Puritans. They were very serious, severe people and they had forbidden many of the country's amusements and pleasures and taken much of the gaiety and colour from life.

"Now that Charles is back we shall have lots of fun again," said one of the people watching the procession pass by.

"Yes. The theatres will re-open, and there will be skating and racing – ."

"And dancing round the maypole on Mayday."

"They call him the Merry Monarch," said a woman in the crowd.

"Too merry, some would think," remarked a man who might have preferred the Puritans. "Still they do say he will encourage science and the pursuit of knowledge too."

"And music."

The only music allowed in the church under Cromwell had been the plain, monotonous, dull singing of psalms. Now back came the organs, the harpsichords, the spinets. Back came the violins, the anthems and the melodies. Back came the singers and, most important of all to Henry, back came the choir of the children of the Chapel Royal.

. . . . .

When Henry was about nine or ten years old, his Uncle Thomas took him along to see Captain Cooke, the master of the children's choir. Captain Cooke listened to his singing, asked him some questions and was quick to note that here was an intelligent boy with an exceptionally clear and pleasing voice. So Henry Purcell became one of the boys of the Chapel Royal. There were twelve in all, aged from about nine to sixteen. They attended a special school where they learned Latin and mathematics and the usual school subjects as well as having lessons on two or three of the musical instruments of the time – the harpsichord or the spinet perhaps, or the lute, violin or organ. Added to this was the daily singing practice of hymns, anthems and sacred songs.

The great day of the week, of course, was Sunday when the boys sang before the King in the Chapel Royal, accompanied often by the men's choir and the great booming organ and twenty-four violinists.

Captain Cooke was a good teacher and a kind and clever man, and the boys were enthusiastic and hard-working. Henry soon made friends and settled very happily into the school. He took great delight in the music and, above all, he enjoyed the singing. He was willing to go on singing for the whole of his life and he often thought that this was what he would do.

Then one day something happened that cast gloom over the boys. They were practising an anthem for Sunday. They had worked and worked on it and brought it near to perfection. Captain Cooke was very pleased.

"That's good," he said. "We'll sing it just once more." The boys waited for his sign and started again. Their voices rang out, clear and beautiful – every one in perfect tune, every one in perfect time.

Then – crack – someone spoiled it. Had he choked, or was he trying to hide a cough? It was a boy called John. His cheeks went scarlet as everyone turned to look at him. Captain Cooke continued conducting as if nothing had happened. The boys went on singing. Only John remained silent for a moment and then cautiously joined in again. He sang well for a few bars. Then his voice came out in a low sort of growl. It was no good trying. He was ruining the choir! He sang no more that week and Captain Cooke gave him some sheets of music to sort out while the others were practising.

"Your voice has broken, John," he said kindly. "I'm sorry. I wasn't expecting it to happen yet. I'm afraid you'll have to leave."

So John left and the boys talked sadly about it for several days, for he had been a specially popular member of the choir.

"He was only just thirteen," said someone. "Robert and Edmund were sixteen when their voices changed."

"Still, it has to happen to us all at some time," put in someone wisely.

"I wonder what John will do now."

"Well, he'll get thirty pounds a year as an ex-choirboy."

"And a gift of clothes."

"What will you do when your voice breaks?" they began to ask each other.

"What will you do, Henry?" said one.

Henry looked bewildered. He knew of course that all boys' voices changed when they were about fourteen or fifteen or sixteen, but he had never really considered it before. It was an awful thought.

"I don't know," he replied. "What will you do?"

"I shall be a builder," said someone. "My father says there's a good future for builders. So much of the city still has to be rebuilt after the fire, and I've heard that Sir Christopher Wren is planning to build a great new cathedral."

They had lived through difficult and frightening times, these boys. In Henry Purcell's short life there had been war with the Dutch. There had been the Great Plague, killing off hundreds and hundreds of people. Then there had been the Great Fire of London, which had destroyed eighty-nine churches and more than thirteen hundred houses.

A small pink-cheeked boy came to take John's place and the school settled back into its normal routine – not that it was ever quite normal, for sometimes the young singers had to perform at London theatres, if it were the King's wish, and sometimes they had to go away for a week or two and sing in other towns.

They were encouraged also to compose their own music and Henry found that he was quite good at this.

He wrote short, sad little pieces that perhaps were connected with his memories of the sickness and sadness of the Plague. He wrote merry dancing pieces and short songs and slow marches that reminded him of processions through the city. He wrote music that seemed to leap and crackle like the flames had done in the Fire of London.

Then when he was twelve he wrote a very special piece of music. He showed it to Captain Cooke who took it away and tried it on the organ. He thought it was remarkable for a boy of twelve.

"This is very good," he told Henry. "We will put some words to it and sing it on the King's birthday."

So, on his birthday, the King received a parchment bearing the title:

> The Address of the Children
> of the Chapel Royal to the King
> on His Majesty's Birthday A.D. 1670

Charles the Second always enjoyed his boy singers and on this special day, singing this special song, their young voices sounded more than usually sweet and clear to him. As for Henry Purcell, it must have been one of the happiest and proudest times of his life. He seemed to have the answer now to the question of what he would do when his voice broke. He would be a composer. He would write music for the church and songs and dance tunes for the theatre.

When his voice did break he was fifteen, but he had already been given two extra duties. He helped the man who kept the royal instruments in good repair. He learned to tune harpsichords and put new strings in worn violins and new hairs in their bows. He mended flutes and recorders and copied out sheets of music. He assisted too in tuning the great organ in Westminster Abbey and mending its bellows and pipes. He was sad to leave the children's choir of the Chapel Royal, but he was hopeful and excited too, for with his talents the whole world of music was open to him.

Success came quickly, for at sixteen he had a song published. This was followed by music of all kinds. He composed it for plays and dances, for orchestras, duets and solos, for church anthems and processions and special occasions. He was very talented, skilful and hard-working and his music had great beauty. It echoed through every church in the land during the reigns of three kings – Charles II, James II and William and Mary. His songs too were sung by ordinary people in the streets. He is still considered by many people to be the greatest of English composers.

And the "Address of the Children of the Chapel Royal on His Majesty's Birthday A.D. 1670" – where is it now? No one knows. It was mislaid or lost long ago. Perhaps it is lying in an old dusty attic somewhere – a roll of faded parchment locked in a box or caught in the back of a drawer. Perhaps one day it will come to light again and we shall once more hear the music that Henry Purcell, the great composer, wrote at the age of twelve.

Choice for Maria

Maria was a novice in the Nonnberg convent at Salzburg in Austria. She was twenty years old and had completed a teacher training course in Vienna. The Nonnberg convent had stood for twelve centuries. It was a beautiful abbey with arched ceilings and worn stone floors and stained glass windows and long, quiet cloisters. Maria loved it all, every stick and stone of it, and in less than a year now she hoped to be accepted into the Benedictine order of nuns and to remain within the walls of Nonnberg for ever. This was her greatest wish and she felt sure it was the will of God.

Then one day the Reverend Mother Abbess sent for her, and to Maria's surprise she seemed to translate the will of God in a different way.

"There is a man living in the nearby village of Aigen who needs our help," she explained. "His name is Baron von Trapp, and his wife died four years ago. He has a large family and one of his little daughters is in poor health and cannot go to school. He asked if we could send a teacher for her." The Reverend Mother paused and Maria knew what was coming next. She wanted to say,

"Oh no, don't send me. I don't want to leave the convent," but she said nothing.

"You will go to his house this afternoon," went on the Reverend Mother. "You will stay till the end of June. Then you will come back. Go my child. Do the work well and do it with your whole heart."

Maria's heart at that moment felt as heavy as lead. Leave Nonnberg? Leave this beautiful place? June was a long way ahead. This was only October. She would be away for nine whole months.

The village of Aigen was about twenty minutes ride by bus out of Salzburg. The Villa Trapp was a large grey house in a big and beautiful garden. It had lawns and flower beds and vegetable plots and its own private wood; and round it spread meadows and trees and beyond them the mountains – the same mountains that Maria had seen from Nonnberg.

That afternoon, a little fearfully, she rang the bell

on the big double oak doors of the house and in a few moments she was meeting the Baron. He welcomed her warmly in the great entrance hall.

"I'm very glad to see you," he said. "I will call the children to meet you."

Baron von Trapp had been the captain of a submarine in the days when Austria had been a larger and more powerful country, with her own navy. He loved the sea and missed it very much and he tried to run his own home as if it were a ship.

"I will call the children," he said to Maria, and to her surprise he took out a whistle and blew a number of different notes and phrases.

"They each know their own sound," he explained. "I find it easier than calling them all by name, when they are in different parts of the house."

Maria expected to hear scampering feet, banging doors and noisy shouts, but the von Trapp family did not come down like that at all. They appeared from various upstairs rooms, formed a neat line on the landing and descended in silence down the stairs. Then they stood before their father, facing him in descending order of height. There were six of them, four girls and two boys. The boys wore white sailor suits. The girls wore white sailor blouses and matching skirts.

"Children, this is our new teacher, Fraulein Maria," said the Baron.

"Good afternoon, Fraulein Maria," chorused the children and each gave a bow, polite and perfect. To Maria it seemed unbelievable, like something out of a book.

"Which is the one I am to teach?" she asked.

"Ah, her name is Maria too, but she is in bed. I will take you up to her."

The Baron led the way upstairs, telling Maria about his little daughter's illnesses as they went. Then after the introduction to the child, he showed her another door, saying,

"This is your room, Fraulein – but tell me, what do you think of my children?"

"They are very well behaved," replied Maria.

"Oh!" said the Baron, "not always, I'm afraid. We've had nurses and governesses and teachers – twenty-five altogether in the last four years. The last one stayed no longer than two months. I hope you will stay longer than that."

"Oh yes," answered Maria. "I shall stay nine months. Then I shall return to the convent."

The Baron glanced at her. She looked too young and pretty to shut herself away from the world behind those thick abbey walls at Nonnberg.

"Perhaps she'll change her mind by then," he thought. But Maria, before she went to bed that night, made herself a calendar showing two hundred and fifty days – the number she would have to spend at the Villa Trapp. She crossed out the first one. She was already one day nearer her return to Nonnberg.

. . . . .

It took a little time to get used to the great big house with all its rooms and all its servants, but Maria quickly made friends with the seven children and also with the housekeeper, who was very kind to her. She enjoyed teaching the little girl, Maria, and also Johanna who was too small to walk the long distance to school. Martina, the baby of the family, was only four, but she too liked to come and listen to the lessons.

The Baron was often away. He seemed a sad man and Maria felt very sorry for him. She felt sorry also for the children. They had this big and beautiful garden and yet they scarcely ever played in it, but merely took walks in it like grown-up people.

"Couldn't they have some play clothes?" she asked the housekeeper. "White sailor suits are so unsuitable for climbing trees or rolling in the grass."

"Oh no," replied the housekeeper. "The Baron wouldn't like it. He likes them to look neat and tidy all the time."

Another thing that puzzled Maria was the way the family divided into three sections. The boys were supposed to keep to their own rooms and the older girls were to keep to theirs. The little girls belonged to the nursery, which was where Maria was expected to be. It seemed strange to her when the older children sometimes knocked at the nursery door and said,

"May we come in for a while?"

"Why can't they play and read and talk all in one room like any other family?" Maria asked the housekeeper. "They only meet at meal times."

"I suppose it's the way the Baron wants it to be," replied the housekeeper. "It's always been like that since I've been here."

But as the days went by it became obvious that the

children liked to be where Fraulein Maria was and they wandered more and more often towards the nursery.

One wet Saturday afternoon when they gathered there, they found that she had a guitar.

"Is it yours, Fraulein?" asked one of the boys.

"Yes, I had it when I was at college."

"Can you play it?"

"Yes. I'll play it and we'll sing, shall we?" She started to play an old Austrian folk-song, a song that she thought everyone would know. The children listened in silence.

"Come on, sing it with me," Maria said.

"We don't know it."

"Well, let's have another one then." She started another, but the children didn't know that either – nor the next, nor the next.

"Tell me something you *do* know," suggested Maria. There was an awkward silence. Then Johanna said, "Silent Night."

Maria played it, and shyly the children joined in – at first only the little ones, then the bigger ones too.

"Oh it sounded lovely," said Agathe, the eldest girl. "Please let's sing it again." So they sang it again and again.

"What else do you know?" asked Maria. "Let's make

a list." Slowly the list grew – two more Christmas carols and a few hymns and the national anthem – but none of the old folk-songs of Austria.

"Oh teach us some please, Fraulein."

So Maria taught them some. The children were quick to learn and they seemed very musical too.

"Let's light the fire in the library and sing there," suggested the boys. So they all moved into the library and gathered round Maria on the soft carpet by the fire. The little girls leaned against her as she played the guitar, the others stared into the dancing flames, and they all sang.

Then suddenly the door opened and in came the Baron, who had been away for several days.

"Father!" cried the children and they ran to greet him. He kissed them all and said,

"Children, you were singing! It sounded wonderful. Do sing again." He joined them on the floor, leaning against one of the big armchairs and hugging Martina, and he listened in delight. "It's wonderful," he kept saying, "it's wonderful."

"Father," said Agathe, "you used to play the violin a long time ago. I remember."

"Oh yes," added Rupert, the eldest boy. "I remember too. I know where it is, Father. Shall I fetch it for you?"

"Oh I don't know. I haven't played it since – . I haven't played it for years."

"Please, Father, please."

"All right. I'll try."

So the children sang and Maria played her guitar and the Baron played his violin. He played it hesitantly at first as if he had forgotten how to play. Then he grew more confident, his fingers loosened and the flames danced and the room was filled with music.

. . . . . .

The weeks passed quickly and Christmas drew near. Austria has a number of old customs associated with Christmas. Some of them the children knew, but others they did not. They did not seem to know much about the Advent wreath.

"Don't you have one every year?" asked Fraulein Maria.

"No. What is it?" demanded the children.

"It's a wreath made of branches from a fir tree. It has four candles fastened to it, one for each Sunday in Advent, and it is hung from the ceiling with four red ribbons."

"And when are the candles lit?"

"One candle is lit on the first Sunday in Advent, and left alight while we sing Christmas carols. Then it is blown out. Two are lit on the second Sunday, three on the third Sunday and four on the fourth Sunday. And when the four candles are burning all together, then everyone knows that Christmas is almost here."

So the family made an Advent wreath and their father hung it from the ceiling of the nursery.

The main Christmas celebrations are held on Holy Eve, or, as we would call it, Christmas Eve. So, early on that evening the children were allowed into the big drawing room, which had been kept locked for the past week. They stood still and gazed in wonder at the tall

Christmas tree reaching to the ceiling and hung with small gifts and little gaily wrapped cakes and sweets, and glowing with a hundred and twenty candles.

Presents were piled on tables standing round the room and what excitement there was as everyone began to open them. Later in the evening Maria went to Nonnberg for Midnight Mass and just as she was leaving the house the Baron said,

"I have dreaded Christmas these last few years, but this year you have made it a very happy time for us. Thank you Fraulein Maria."

Maria had been to the convent on all her days off and she felt very happy to be there in the ancient church again on Holy Eve. It was like coming home. She tried to fix her thoughts on holy things, but for once she found it rather difficult, because she kept thinking of the children and the Christmas tree and Baron von Trapp's words of gratitude.

Time passed and Easter came, with chocolate Easter eggs and marzipan ones and painted ones hidden in the garden for the children to find – put there, the little ones believed, by the Easter Rabbit. Spring came and the beginning of summer – May and June. June was a beautiful month but it brought a feeling of sadness and insecurity. The children knew only too well that Fraulein Maria would be leaving them at the end of the month and returning to Nonnberg to become a nun. They knew that she had only been lent to them, but they longed for her to stay.

"Why can't she stay with us always?" asked Johanna when the children were talking to their father on Maria's day off.

"Because she's going to be a nun," explained Rupert.

"I want her to stay," protested little Martina with tears in her eyes.

"Father," said Agathe, "there's only one thing to do to try and make Fraulein Maria stay with us."

"Yes, Agathe, and what's that?"

"You must marry her and make her our mother." Father smiled.

"I'd love to do that," he said, "but I don't even know whether she likes me well enough to agree."

"Fraulein Maria," the younger ones asked her the next day, "do you like Father?"

"Of course I like him," she replied in an absent-minded way, and she was puzzled when they went rushing off at once, shouting,

"It's all right, Father. She does like you. She said so."

Her calendar showed that there were only twelve days left now before she would return to the convent to be received into it for as long as she wished to stay. Yet that very same evening the Baron looked earnestly into her eyes and said,

"The children told me you will accept my offer."

"What offer?"

"I want to marry you." There was a long silence. Maria was utterly bewildered.

"But I can't marry you. I'm going back to the convent. You know I am."

"Please. The children all love you so much."

"I love them too, but I'm going to be received into Nonnberg. It's the will of God."

"Is it the will of God? Might it not perhaps be the will of God that you should stay here with us and be a mother to the children?"

"Oh, I don't know. I don't know."

A few minutes later, Maria was running by the river through the still June evening, running, running to Nonnberg. She would ask to see the Reverend Mother Abbess. She would ask her what she ought to do. Reverend Mother would know the will of God. Maria would accept whatever she said, however hard it might be.

. . . . .

So it happened that instead of being received as a nun into the Benedictine order, Maria was married to the Baron in the ancient church of Nonnberg. She wore a white frock and a flowing veil kept in place by a circlet of edelweiss. The whole community of nuns was there, and so too were the seven children – filled with joy and happiness.

Adapted from the book
The Trapp Family Singers
by Maria Augusta Trapp,
published by Geoffrey Bles.

The Boy Who Never Was

The people of the Netherlands have always had to fight against the sea. Two-fifths of their land is below sea-level, and even as long ago as the first century A.D. they were piling up banks of earth against the shore.

Many times the sea has rushed inland and swept away whole villages and farms and fields. Many times the Dutch people have built and rebuilt their banks of earth. These are called dykes, and they hold back the grey North Sea. Today they stretch a very long way and form a strong defence against high tides and storms.

There have been many stories of bravery in these low-lying lands, but the story that is best known is not true at all.

Nearly everyone knows the story of "Pieter and the Dyke" but not many people know that it was written by an American lady about 1865. Her name was Mary Mapes Dodge and she wrote the story as part of a book called *Hans Brinkman or The Silver Skates*.

The story tells how a boy called Pieter was walking home one afternoon along the road beside a dyke. It was winter time and it was already beginning to get dark. Pieter noticed a thin trickle of water running down the side of the dyke. He saw that it was coming through a tiny hole. He could hear the sea beating against the other side and he knew it would soon rush in and break down the dyke and flood the town.

What could he do? There was no one else in sight, and if he ran to get help precious time would be lost. He knelt down and put his finger in the tiny hole. It just fitted and stopped the water coming through.

He hoped and hoped that someone would soon come along and see him, but no one came. So there Pieter stayed all night, kneeling on the road with his finger in the dyke.

In the morning, when people started going to their work, the brave boy was found. He was tired and hungry, and stiff with cold, but he had saved the town.

Of course, one little boy's finger could not possibly win a battle against the strength of the sea. All the same, most people believed the story and those who visited the Netherlands nearly always asked the same questions –

"Where did Pieter live?"

"Where is the actual dyke?"

"It's only a story," they were told.

Years went by and people began to travel more and more. Those who went to the Netherlands still asked the same questions –

"Where did Pieter live?"

"Where is the actual dyke?"

At last the Dutch people put up a statue to satisfy the tourists. It shows Pieter kneeling down with his finger in the dyke. He is looking back over his shoulder as if hoping for someone to come and help him.

One of the Dutch princesses unveiled the statue in the year 1950 and there it stands for all to see. It honours Pieter, the boy who never was, but it also honours all young people who help in "the struggle of the Netherlands against the water".

William the Guillemot

The word guillemot comes from Guillaume, the French for William, which explains the reason for the name of the bird in this story.

William the guillemot was a handsome bird, very dark brown with white chest and underparts and a slim black bill. He was a bird of the open ocean and came near to land only at the breeding season. His mate at this moment was perched on a cliff ledge keeping her single egg warm, in company with hundreds of other birds of her kind as well as with razorbills and kittiwakes.

William shared the work with her, but now he was taking his turn at fishing and diving a little way out at sea. He had caught and eaten enough fish to satisfy him and he was diving now just for the sheer pleasure of it. Nothing could describe the joy of a dive, nine and a half metres down through the surging, salt waves. He could stay down longer than a minute and then shoot up again, damp and fresh and glistening.

Ah well! It was time to relieve his mate once more, or perhaps to sit with her for a while and join in the general gossip, and proudly guard the brownish, whitish egg. The egg was pear-shaped so that there was less chance of it falling off the ledge and breaking, though this happened often enough with one bird or another.

William flew towards the land where the rugged cliffs towered up against the grey sky. Every jagged ledge was covered with birds. The number, and the noise, was unbelievable. There were razorbills and kittiwakes and hundreds of guillemots. They sat closely together, side by side with their backs to the sea – whole walls of birds, one wall above the other over the face of the cliff. Some birds were landing, some were leaving, others were balancing, bullying, fluttering, flying, screeching, screaming, croaking, quarrelling. Their raucous cries drowned even the roar of the waves against the rocks and the booming echoes of both birds and sea. Many of the birds were brooding eggs between their feet. Some already had young ones, grey downy little creatures, staring out in surprise at life.

There was William's mate. Another bird had moved up closer to her and taken William's place, so there was a good deal of pushing and screaming to do before he could edge back into his rightful position. Then it was that he saw fragments of broken egg shell and a small grey ball of damp fluff blinking in a shaft of sunlight. The egg had hatched and young Bill had arrived.

. . . . .

Now, life became earnest indeed. Young Bill had to be protected against the fierce gulls that swooped round the cliffs, liking nothing better than a meal of a helpless baby guillemot. The parent birds took turns at guarding him and fetching fish for him to eat. He sat facing the cliff, snuggled against one parent's warm body, and when the other parent returned with a fish in its bill he greeted it with loud shrieks of hunger and joy. When Bill was only two weeks old, William and his mate decided to leave the cliff ledge and take to the sea, as many hundreds of other birds and their young were doing. The gulls were such a menace that the cliff home had become a very dangerous place indeed.

Bill had grown quickly and was already about half the size of his parents. His wing feathers had not grown big enough to support him yet, but his body feathers were now waterproof and he would swim without any difficulty. First he had to jump from the cliff to the sea. This took great courage and William and his mate called and persuaded and even pushed him a little until at last he gave a brave leap and hurtled down, fluttering his tiny wings and descending into the sea. His parents were at his side in a moment, fighting off a hopeful gull and leading their young one further and further away from the land.

He swam and dived without any teaching, but his parents continued to feed him for several weeks as the three of them wandered over the sea. Then one day, able to fish for himself, able to fly and eager to explore, Bill joined a passing group of young birds like himself and flew away with them to lead his own life.

Now William could concentrate again on catching fish just for himself. He could dive once more just for the sheer pleasure of it – nine and a half metres down through the surging, salt waves. He could stay down longer than a minute and then shoot up again, damp and fresh and glistening. What could be better? What could be happier than the life of a guillemot? He dived and dived with joy.

Early one morning, far out at sea, an oil tanker called *Delphi* was in trouble. She had run aground on a reef and was listing heavily.

"Mayday! Mayday!" she radioed for help.

The Navy and the department of trade at once went into action to save her, and to save if possible her valuable cargo of oil. Once this was released, it seemed probable that she might be refloated.

Some of the crew were lifted off by helicopter. An empty tanker drew near and some of the *Delphi*'s oil was pumped into it. This improved the position a little. More oil was transferred.

"A few more tonnes," said the *Delphi*'s captain, "and we'll be able to refloat her."

Then a storm arose. High winds and wildly beating waves prevented any further transfer of oil. At the same time it became obvious that one of the *Delphi*'s tanks had been holed, as a slow stream of thick black oil seeped out on to the reef and down into the sea. Blown by strong winds and swept along by the tide, the ever growing pool of oil began a journey of its own, nearer and nearer to the place where the guillemots and razorbills were swimming and diving and feeding in a calmer sea.

William was among them, free and fearless and contented. He noticed nothing unusual. He smelled nothing strange. Even his instinct gave him no warning of danger. The great black oil slick floated nearer and nearer – nearer and nearer to the helpless and unsuspecting birds.

Suddenly they saw it. They smelled it. They felt it. The thick, murky liquid surrounded them. It blinded them. It covered them. The first William knew of it was the moment when he rose to the surface from a dive, and instead of inhaling a deep draught of fresh sea air, he choked and gasped and floundered in a terrifying black pool of oil. For a few minutes he struggled and struggled. His wings beat wildly. He could not fly. He could not swim. Black oil blinded him. It seeped into every crevice between his feathers. It coated every part of his head and body. He was helpless. There was nothing he could do. With hundreds of other birds he drifted for hours on the tide, and when evening came he was washed up on the beach more dead than alive.

. . . . . .

The *Delphi* was an innocent victim of disaster. There are many others like her, tankers whose oil cargoes flood the seas, wrecked ships whose own engine oil escapes, even unscrupulous sailors who clean out their tanks near the shore. It is a tragedy that is repeated again and again, bringing death to thousands and thousands of sea birds around the coasts.

Fortunately there are also people who search the beaches day after day, and work tirelessly to save at least some of the birds.

William the guillemot was lucky. Next morning three people walked along the beach, glancing despairingly at the scores of dead birds washed in by the tide, and noticing hopefully any that appeared to have a spark of life left in them. William made a feeble movement and was at once picked up and placed in a plastic bag with only his head left out. The bag was bound quite lightly to prevent him from fluttering, and he was placed, like a parcel, into a cardboard box with numbers of other birds, similarly wrapped.

He did not know what happened to him after that, but he was put into a van and driven a long way to a building among green fields. Then the van stopped and the boxes were lifted down.

"Oh poor things, poor things," said someone, and box after box was carried inside. For some of the birds help was already too late, but for William, fortunately, it had come in time. An elastic band was slipped round his beak and gentle hands removed the wrappings and held him over a sink. A special detergent was rubbed thoroughly into his feathers and the oil was squeezed out, bit by bit.

There were several workers in the room. The man in charge was an expert at the job, but the others were volunteers – local people and one or two school children. They had learned how to hold the birds gently but firmly, so that they could not flap their wings.

Even when most of the oil was out, William felt very

ill and very sorry for himself. Then came the pleasant part of the treatment. He was put under a small shower so that the detergent was rinsed away. His spirits were lifted a little, as the fresh water came splashing over him, and he fluffed out his feathers to take full advantage of it.

Next the band was removed from his beak, and he was put in a warm room to dry, and later he was taken to another room where there was a large tank of salt water. There were a number of other birds there. Some were swimming happily, but others quickly scrambled out and stood at the side because their own natural oils had not yet recovered enough to keep them afloat. William managed fairly well, and in a few days he felt bright enough to accept a few strips of raw fish.

. . . . . .

A few weeks later a car drove down to the coast, carrying boxes of birds ready to be released. They could not go to the beach where they had been found, for the water there was not yet clean and pure enough, so they were taken further along the shore in the same general area.

William felt bewildered, pressed so tightly against the other birds and jogging along so strangely in the car. Then his box was lifted out and opened and he stepped out on to the shingle. A breath of salt air filled his lungs. This was wonderful. It was a smell he had almost forgotten. There was a familiar noise around him too – the cry of guillemots and razorbills as they were released in twos and threes. Some trotted down the beach, others tried their wings and others plunged into the sea.

For a few moments William was uncertain what to do. Then he made for the sea. He swam and swam further and further out. Then he dived nine and a half metres down through the surging, salt waves. A minute later he shot up again, damp and fresh and glistening. The oil, the discomfort, the fear were forgotten. He dived and dived and dived with joy.

The Blizzard

Mr Roberts never found it very easy to get the full attention of the second year French class, and today he felt he was fighting a losing battle. It was the first period after dinner, when a number of children seemed half asleep anyway, but the more alert ones were fascinated by the colour of the sky.

"Sir, isn't it dark?"

"Look, the sky's yellow!"

"Shall I switch the lights on?"

The classroom lights made the atmosphere seem more eerie than ever, and then the snow began. It fell against the windows in large feathery flakes that slid down the glass and in a few moments began to bank up against the corners of the frames.

"It's snowing!"

"Look at it!"

"It's settling already."

"Ugh! I've got to cycle through this."

Mr Roberts gave up the struggle for a while and joined the children in simply staring out of the window. Now the air was filled with the whirling snowflakes, blown by a wind that had sprung up from nowhere, so that as much snow appeared to be going up as coming down. Already the trees were holding out their arms to receive the white benediction. Already the branches were glistening and beautiful.

"It's settling quickly. It's quite thick already."

"What a pity the lunch break's over. We could have had a snowball fight."

French was far from everyone's thoughts now. One boy was planning to build a snowman for his little brother. A girl was deciding to run straight home instead of calling at the library on the way, as she had planned. A boy was wishing he had left his bicycle at home and another was wishing he had brought his to school. Someone was hoping her mother was not out with the baby; and a girl called Clare was thinking about her father's sheep. She lived on a farm and the sheep were on the hillside, which that very morning had looked so green and sunny. If the snow went on for long her father would probably think it wise to bring the sheep down to the lower field.

"I wish I could go home and help him," thought Clare. She alone realised the problems and difficulties that snow could bring. The other children, mostly town-dwellers, felt excited and restless and longed to go out in it.

The classroom door opened and a girl entered.

"Will the children for the south-bound bus come now please," she said.

"Coo! They're going home early."

"Aren't they lucky?"

About six children gathered up their books and papers, quickly packed their bags and hurried to the cloakroom for their coats and jackets. Clare was among them. In about five minutes, boys and girls from other classes had joined them and they had all climbed cheerfully on to the bus.

"It's a different driver."

"Where's Mr Bernard?"

"It's too early for him," explained the driver. "I'm just a relief. The snow's pretty thick out in the country and we thought we'd better get you lot safely home before it got any worse."

"Mm. Good, isn't it?"

"Nice and early."

"Bet the others are envious."

The bus chugged into life and the journey began, along one or two town streets and into the country. There the snow was much more in evidence than it had been around the school. Fields were white and hedges and trees were laden. Snow lay deeply on the road, becoming deeper as the bus advanced. The windscreen wipers worked at a frantic speed, pushing veritable banks of snow off the glass. Visibility became swiftly worse as the whole view was filled with whirling, swirling snowflakes surging in misty clouds round the bus.

The first stop was at a group of cottages not far out of town. Three girls and a boy alighted there, waved to their friends and disappeared from sight. The bus went on and conditions rapidly grew worse.

"I'll have the whole afternoon to help Dad with the sheep," thought Clare with satisfaction.

"A real blizzard, isn't it?" said the boy beside her.

"It's drifting too. Look, someone's abandoned his car." The car stood coldly by the roadside, with snow banked up beside it. Soon there was another in a similar position. Then there were two heavy lorries, with deep wheel tracks still visible, showing the great efforts that had been made to keep the vehicles on the road.

The bus driver was worried. He was not very familiar with this route and he did not normally drive a school bus. He felt the responsibility of this crowd of children lying somewhat heavily upon him. He understood that all but two of them had to be dropped at the village. Grimly he clung to the steering wheel and peered half blindly ahead. Then suddenly he found the way entirely blocked. A great drift of snow was lying across the road, blown into a long high barrier, with wind ripples marking it as if the sea had washed that way.

"Go on, go on," shouted some of the children encouragingly, as the driver tried to control the shuddering wheels.

"Shall we get out and push?" asked others.

"No. Stay where you are." The driver jumped down and looked round anxiously. The position was hopeless. The children would be stuck here for the rest of the day, probably all night. All he could do would be to wait and hope that some form of help might eventually get through to him. He broke the news to the children. They did not seem unduly disturbed. Some indeed, became quite excited. Some, very sensibly, began to do their homework.

Clare was about to do the same, when she had an idea. She knew where a footpath led up the hillside at this particular point. It cut off the village entirely. It went up over the hill and down the other side to her own farm. It would lead her right home.

"Will it be all right if I get out?" she asked the driver. "I know where there's a footpath just along here on the right. It's a short cut to my farm – well, not a *short* cut – but it leads to our house. I could get my mother to phone the police for you and tell them about the bus being stranded."

It seemed a good idea, but the driver was doubtful. Ought he to let a girl go walking off on her own?

"Are you sure you know the way?" he asked.

"Oh yes. I've been there before – in the summer."

"How old are you?"

"Just on thirteen."

"How long will it take you?"

"About half an hour – well, about three-quarters of an hour, I should think."

A rather small eleven-year-old girl came up to the front.

"I can go that way too," she said. "I live near Clare – well, fairly near." Her name was Meg, and the last thing *she* wanted to do was to shiver all night in a snowed-up bus.

Again the driver hesitated. Well, two were better than one, he supposed. They seemed sensible children.

"All right," he agreed slowly. "Keep together then, and phone directly you reach home." He pressed the lever that slid back the door. Clare and Meg stepped down amid a chorus of farewells and a few cheers. The children pressed their faces to the windows and peered into the blizzard. Almost at once, Clare and Meg were swallowed up in the mist.

"Lucky things," said someone enviously.

"Oh I don't know. I'd rather stay here and see the fun."

"Not much fun. We might be here all night."

"We might indeed," thought the driver anxiously.

Meanwhile Meg and Clare plodded up the hillside, clambering round rocks, slipping and sliding, plunging at times into deep pockets of snow, battling always with a whirl of snowflakes that stung their faces like a host of tiny, freezing daggers. Both children secretly began to wonder if it might not have been wiser to stay in the bus.

"Are you all right?" asked Clare, as Meg fell down for the fifth time.

"Mm," she panted, rubbing her cold hands together. "It's going to take us a long time."

"Yes. It's such a struggle. Never mind." Bravely they set off again, no breath for conversation, no energy for anything but plodding upward and upward, and then, at long last, downward and downward, slipping and sliding, and fighting the blizzard. They were heartened by the knowledge that they were getting nearer home. They both knew this part of the journey well, but familiar landmarks were obscured by snow and there was a little secret panic when they could not find the place where a footpath led down to the cottage where Meg lived.

"It's here somewhere. It must be."

"We might have passed it."

"Surely not. It must be further on."

"Everything looks so different."

The cottage itself was never visible from that point because the ground dropped away steeply further down. In any case, the landscape was hidden in a curtain of mist.

"You know where my path leaves yours, don't you?" said Meg. "There's a big rock, with a tiny fir tree growing out from underneath it."

"Yes, I know. We'd better walk back a bit."

"Seems awful to go back."

"Keep close together."

They retraced their steps. It seemed a dreadful waste of precious time but Clare did not like to send Meg stumbling down among rocks and bushes unless she knew she were on the right path.

"This could be it," Clare said after a while, coming across a hump of snow. They tore at it with their ice-cold hands and bit by bit the branches of a small fir tree appeared.

"Yes. It is," agreed Meg. "Thanks Clare. I'll soon be home now."

"Do you think you'll be all right on your own?"

"Yes thanks."

They stood still a moment, panting and resting.

"Meg," said Clare. "You'll be home before I shall. I think you'd better do the phoning."

"We're not on the phone."

"Oh. It's up to me then."

"Do you think the other children will be there all night?" asked Meg. "They'll be very cold and hungry."

"No, I think a snow-plough or a bulldozer will

reach them when the phone message gets through. We shall hear all about it tomorrow, I expect. Goodbye then Meg. Good luck."

"Goodbye. Good luck to you, too."

Clare watched her small, struggling figure disappear into the blizzard. Her cottage was not far now and she soon reached home safely. Clare, meanwhile, still had a good way to go. The path was very steep and at times she found it easier to sit down and slide jerkily on her way. It was still early in the afternoon. Her mother would be surprised to see her home so soon. She was thinking longingly of evening by the big log fire in the farmhouse when she came suddenly upon a small group of sheep huddled in the snow. She spread her arms wide and shouted at them,

"Down. Go down." Two of them were already half buried in the snow and had a job to scramble to their cold, stiff legs. Once on their feet, however, they were quicker than Clare at finding the most direct route down.

There were some more.

"Down, down," said Clare.

One had settled itself in the shelter of a rock a little to the left. It seemed unwilling to be helped. Clare went over to it, each leg going deeply, deeply into the snow.

"Go on. Go down. Down," she cried and the wind whipped snow into her mouth as she opened it.

She did not quite know what happened next. The sheep scrambled to its feet, stumbled and gave a nervous "baa". At the same time there was a great noise behind her – a noise like the thundering hooves of stampeding cattle. She took a frightened glance backwards at what appeared to be a wall of snow descending upon her. She was knocked off her feet and swept down the hillside. At one moment she saw the sheep turning over and over below her and felt herself being tossed like a stone, down and down and down. At the next moment she had lost consciousness and had become a part of the descending avalanche.

When she regained her senses, Clare was in a state of utter bewilderment. She was icy cold and most uncomfortable. There seemed to be a great weight on her body, crushing, crushing her. Breathing was difficult and her heart was full of fear. She was lying on her back, with her arms pinned forwards on her chest. She thought she must be dreaming, for she was going through the same struggling terror of trying to wake up that she had occasionally experienced during a nightmare.

This was not a dream. She knew suddenly and clearly that she was buried under the snow and that she was wide awake. She had sometimes helped her father to dig out sheep that had been buried. Now she was buried herself. An avalanche! The wall of snow that had knocked her off her feet and carried her down the hillside, must have been an avalanche. She thought avalanches belonged to countries like Austria and Switzerland. How was she going to get out? How was she going to breathe? She strained every muscle and tried to push the load of hard packed snow off her body. She could not move it.

The snow that rested on her hands felt rather strange – not cold and icy and wet, but almost warm, almost woolly. And what was this on her face? It felt like a small current of air. She realised that a sheep was lying on top of her, pressed closely against her, its mouth close to her own. By good fortune, its breathing had melted the snow and formed a tiny shaft of air – a breathing hole above its head. As long as Clare kept still she could share in it. But how long would it be before it froze again?

Fear took hold of her and filled her mind with tormenting thoughts. How long would it be before she was found? Only Meg and the bus driver and the school children knew she had come this way. How long would it be before one of them mentioned the fact? It might be too late. She was overcome by panic. The weight of the sheep and the snow was pressing down on her. It was crushing her. She was afraid. She was terribly afraid.

She tried to control her thoughts. She must think of something else. Sing a hymn to herself. Say some poetry to herself. She found herself saying French – silly little rhymes she had learned in the first year.

> "Sur le pont
> D'Avignon
> On y dansent – "

She forgot what she was trying to say, and she started another –

> "Frère Jacques
> Frère Jacques

Dormez-vous?

Dormez-vous?"

She remembered a boy called Ben insisting that it meant "Friar Jacques, Friar Jacques". Of course it didn't. It meant "brother". Everyone knew that "frère" meant "brother". Clare must have dropped off to sleep at that point or perhaps lost consciousness and sunk into blessed oblivion for a while.

Suddenly she was awake again, feeling weak and strange and excitedly aware that something was moving above her. No, it wasn't the sheep. It was something above the ground. Dimly, as if from far away, she heard a dog barking. It must be her own dog, Jock. Jock was the only dog around here. Perhaps, perhaps –

It was! It was Jock. Half crazy with excitement he was digging with his front paws. He was barking, barking, and Father was helping now with a spade. The disturbed snow was tumbling in and being pushed aside. Father was pulling the sheep to safety, and the sheep was bleating a hymn of thankfulness.

"There's more than one here," said Father to Jock. Jock knew that well enough, but unlike Father he knew that the second rescue was not for a sheep but for his own young mistress, Clare.

"Clare!" cried Father in utter amazement. "How did you get here? I was looking for sheep."

Clare was in no fit state to explain just then but she did draw sufficient breath to murmur,

"Phone police – school bus stranded – other side of village – by Mark's Wood." Then she knew nothing else until she found herself in her own bed, with Mother standing beside her, holding a hot drink and looking relieved because she was awake and moving.

The Story of Joseph

The story of Joseph is told in the Hebrew Bible, the holy book of the Jews and in the Christian Bible. It is told also in the Koran, the holy book of the Muslims.

. . . . . .

There was once a man called Jacob, who lived in the land of Canaan. He had a large family of boys and girls. He loved them all dearly but he could not hide the fact that the one he loved the most was Joseph. This made the brothers jealous of Joseph, especially as he was a dreamy boy who sometimes gave the impression of being rather conceited. The brothers often grumbled to each other about their father's favouritism, and one day when he gave Joseph a new coat they could not contain their jealousy. It was a beautiful coat of many colours, a much better coat than any of the other boys had ever had.

"It's not fair," they grumbled to each other, and some of them hardly ever spoke civilly to their young brother after that, but Joseph seemed scarcely to notice their enmity.

"Do you know what I dreamed last night?" he said one day. "I dreamed that we boys were all in the field binding up sheaves of corn, and my sheaf of corn stood upright, and your sheaves all gathered round it and bowed to it."

"Conceited thing," muttered the brothers. "I suppose you think we shall all bow down to you one day."

A little later, Joseph told them another dream.

"Do you know what I dreamed last night?" he said. "I dreamed that the sun and the moon and eleven stars in the sky bowed down to me."

This made his brothers angrier than ever, and even Jacob, the father, spoke sternly to Joseph.

"Do you think your mother and I and all your brothers are going to bow down to you?" he asked, but to himself he thought, "he's a good boy and a clever one. Perhaps he will become an important man one day. Perhaps his dreams are foretelling a great future for him."

Now Joseph was about seventeen at this time and the brothers were grown men – Reuben, Simeon, Judah and the rest – all but Benjamin who was the youngest of all and still a boy. Joseph was often allowed to stay at home with Benjamin while the older boys had to go and work on their father's land or look after his sheep. One day when they had taken the sheep to new pastures, Jacob said to Joseph,

"Go and see if everything is all right with your brothers and the sheep, and then come back and tell me." So Joseph set off over the hillside and across the fields.

The brothers saw him from the distance.

"Look who's coming," said one.

"That dreamer," said another. "Let's get rid of him." They began to talk wickedly about how it could be done.

"Let's kill him and throw him into a pit."

"We can tell our father that a wild beast attacked him."

"No, no, we mustn't kill him," said Reuben. "Throw him into the pit and leave him there."

Meanwhile Joseph was coming nearer, walking along happily in his coat of many colours. Then his brothers rushed upon him, pulled off his coat and pushed him down into the pit. Hardly had they done so when a company of merchants came that way. They rode on camels and were carrying spices to sell in Egypt.

"Quickly," said Judah. "Let's pull him out again

and offer him to these merchants. They might give us money for him." So Joseph was sold to the merchants for twenty pieces of silver and he was carried away to the land of Egypt.

The brothers killed a young goat and dipped Joseph's coat of many colours in its blood and took it home to their father.

"Look what we found," they said. Jacob stared at it in horror.

"It is Joseph's coat!" he cried. "A wild beast must have killed him." He was bowed down with sorrow and all his sons and all his daughters tried to comfort him, but he mourned and wept and would not be comforted.

. . . . . .

Now although Joseph was so unpopular with his brothers he was in fact a good, honest, hard-working young man and other people usually liked him. When he reached Egypt he was sold as a slave to a man named Potiphar, who was a captain of the guard. Potiphar found that Joseph was no ordinary slave, and he soon became very fond of him. He worked well and was so reliable that after a short time Potiphar put him in charge of the whole household. Everything prospered and went smoothly until Potiphar's wife tried to persuade Joseph to do wrong things. When she found that she could not tempt him in any way she became angry and began to tell lies to her husband about him. Unfortunately Potiphar believed her, and he was so angry and disappointed that he sent Joseph to prison.

Again Joseph showed himself to be a pleasant and useful young man and soon the keeper of the prison gave him charge of the other prisoners. Among them was the king's wine-server, who had offended the king in some way. One morning this man said to Joseph,

"I had a strange dream last night."

"What was it?" asked Joseph.

"I was standing by a grape vine," began the man, "and it had three branches. As I looked, buds appeared on the branches and opened at once into blossom. Then the blossoms turned into grapes, hanging in ripe clusters. In the dream, I picked the grapes, crushed them into the king's cup and handed the cup to him as I used to do."

"I can interpret the dream for you," offered Joseph. "The three branches are three days. In three days the king will send for you and release you from prison and make you his wine-server again. Then you will hand him his cup of wine as you did before."

"Do you think so?" asked the man with pleasure.

"Oh yes," replied Joseph, "and when you are free please think about me and mention me to the king. I was stolen and carried away from my own country, and I have done nothing wrong that I should be kept in prison."

"I will remember," promised the wine-server.

Three days later it was the king's birthday and he gave a feast for his servants. He released his wine-server from prison and the man handed the king his cup of wine as before. So Joseph's prophecy was fulfilled, but the wine-server forgot his promise to Joseph and Joseph remained in prison.

Two years later Pharaoh the king had a dream. He

dreamed he was standing by a river and out of it came seven cows. They were plump and well-fed and they began to browse in the meadow. Then seven more cows came up out of the river. These were thin and bony and they began to eat the plump, well-fed cows. Then Pharaoh awoke.

A little later he fell asleep again and had another dream. This time he dreamed that seven ears of corn grew upon one stalk. They were plump and good and ready to harvest. Then seven thin ears grew up beside them and began to devour the good ears. Then Pharaoh awoke.

In the morning he remembered the two dreams and was puzzled. He sent for his wise men and asked them to explain the meaning of the dreams, but not one of them could interpret them for him. Then he sent for all the magicians of Egypt and told them his dreams, but not one of them could interpret them for him. The wine-server heard what was going on in the palace, and at last he remembered Joseph and told Pharaoh about him.

"He would understand and explain your dreams," he said.

So Pharaoh sent for Joseph and told him the dreams, saying:

"In my dream, I stood upon the bank of a river, and

out of it there came seven fat, well-fed cows, and browsed in the meadow. Then seven more cows came up out of the river after them. These were the thinnest cows I have ever seen in all Egypt, yet the thin cows ate up the fat cows. In the same night I had another dream. I dreamed that seven good, plump ears of corn grew upon one stalk, and after them sprung up seven more ears of corn, thin and withered by the east wind. Then the thin ears devoured the fat ears. I told these dreams to my wise men and to all the magicians of Egypt but not one of them could explain them to me."

"Oh Pharaoh, God is warning you what is going to happen," replied Joseph. "Both dreams have the same meaning. Both dreams are as one. The seven good cows are seven good years, and the seven good ears of corn are the same. The seven thin cows are seven bad years, and the seven withered ears of corn are the same. Egypt will have seven years of plenty through the land and they will be followed by seven years of famine. The famine will be so great that the years of plenty will be almost forgotten.

"I advise you, oh Pharaoh, to choose a man who is discreet and wise and put him in charge of the land. Let him appoint officers to help him and let them gather corn and food during the seven good years and put it in store-houses in readiness for the seven bad years. Let there be store-houses on the land and in the cities. Then when the years of famine come there will be food for all."

Pharaoh thought long and deeply about this.

"Who is there more wise and discreet than this man Joseph?" he asked his servants and counsellors. So he called again for Joseph and said to him,

"I will set you over all the land of Egypt. You will rule my people. Only I, Pharaoh, shall be greater than you." He gave Joseph clothes of fine linen and put a gold chain about his neck. He took his own ring from his finger and put it on Joseph's hand. He gave him a chariot to ride in, and the people bowed down to him as he rode past.

So Joseph settled happily in Egypt and married a young Egyptian woman who bore him two sons. The seven years of plenty came as he had foretold. Crops grew in abundance and the vines were heavy with grapes. Sheep and cattle grew fat and strong and there was far more food than the people could possibly use. Joseph had great store-houses prepared and he chose men to gather in supplies of everything that could be preserved. During each of the seven good years he did this, until the store-houses were overflowing and the country was ready to face misfortune.

Then began the years of famine. Crops withered and died and no grapes grew on the vines. Sheep and cattle grew thin and weak. People became hungry and cried to Pharaoh for bread.

"Go to Joseph," he told them. "He will tell you what to do." So Joseph opened the great store-houses and sold food to the people. Not only was there a famine in Egypt, but there was famine everywhere else too, so that people from other countries came to Egypt to buy corn.

In Joseph's old home in Canaan his father and brothers and sisters were getting short of food too. Their crops had withered and faded, and no grapes grew on their vines. Their cattle had grown thin and died. Their wives and husbands and children were hungry. Jacob, the father, was an old man now, still sad because he had lost Joseph, his favourite son. One day he said to the brothers,

"I have heard that there is corn for sale in Egypt. Go and buy some before we all starve." So the ten elder brothers took donkeys and provisions and went to Egypt, but Jacob would not let Benjamin, the youngest, go.

"Some harm might befall him," he said, remembering Joseph.

Now Joseph himself sometimes helped to serve the people who came to buy corn and it so happened that he was doing this on the day that his ten brothers arrived in Egypt. He recognised them at once but they did not know him. He spoke roughly to them saying,

"What do you want? Where have you come from?"

"We have come from the land of Canaan to buy food," they replied, and they all bowed down to him as Joseph's dream had foretold long ago.

"I think you are spies," said Joseph. "You have come to see what conditions are like in this land."

"No, no, my lord," protested the brothers. "We have come to buy food. We are all brothers. We are not spies."

"I think you are spies," repeated Joseph.

"No, no, my lord. We are all sons of one man – twelve brothers we are."

"Twelve?"

"One brother is dead and the youngest stayed at home with our father."

"Then I wish to see your youngest brother so that I know whether you are speaking the truth or not. I will keep one of you here till you return with your youngest brother."

The brothers looked anxiously at each other, but

Simeon consented to remain behind. Then Joseph ordered his servants to fill the men's sacks and to give them food for the journey – food for themselves and for their donkeys. He also told his servants to put their money back secretly – each man's money in his own sack. So the brothers started on their return journey, and Joseph was filled with sorrow and happiness and a longing to see his father again.

The ten brothers spent the night at an inn on the way home, and when one of them opened his sack to take out some food for the donkeys he saw his own money lying there.

"Look!" he said. "My money has been put in the top of my sack," and he was puzzled and worried about it.

When the brothers at last reached home again with their donkeys and the sacks of corn, Jacob saw at once that Simeon was not with them.

"Where is Simeon?" he asked.

"The lord of the land spoke roughly to us," they explained. "He thought we were spies and he told us to take our youngest brother next time we go. Then he will release Simeon."

"Benjamin shall not go," protested Jacob. "We have already lost Joseph and perhaps Simeon. How can we risk letting Benjamin go?" As they talked, they undid the sacks and each brother found that his money had been returned. Far from being pleased about it, they were worried and afraid.

Time passed and the famine continued, and soon Jacob's family had eaten all the corn they had brought from Egypt.

"You will have to go again and buy some more," Jacob told his sons.

"We cannot go without Benjamin," Judah reminded him. "We shall not be given any corn and Simeon will not be set free."

"Why ever did you tell the man you had another brother?" asked Jacob.

"He accused us of being spies. How were we to know he would ask for our youngest brother?"

"Benjamin shall not go," insisted Jacob.

"But Father, we have almost no food left. Our children are hungry. We shall all starve."

Jacob was in despair, but what could he do? At last he agreed that Benjamin should go.

"Take back the money that was returned to you," he told his sons, "and take these gifts to give the lord of the land – a little honey and some nuts and spices and myrrh. Bring back Simeon and take care of Benjamin. God have mercy on us and keep you all safe."

So once again the brothers and their donkeys came to Egypt and to the great store-house where the corn was being sold. Joseph saw them coming, so he went out of sight and told the steward of his house to ask them to eat with him at noon. When the steward met the brothers and took them to Joseph's house, they offered the money to him and explained about finding it in their sacks.

"Don't worry," said the steward kindly. "We knew about it and meant you to have it." He saw that they had their youngest brother with them so he brought Simeon out to them. He gave them water to wash themselves and he gave food to their donkeys.

When Joseph came back into his house at noon, his brothers still did not recognise him, and they all bowed low to him. He saw that Benjamin was with them and he longed to embrace him, but he had planned to play one more trick upon them. He asked about their home and their father.

"Is he still alive?"

"Yes, my lord."

"Is he in good health?"

"Yes, my lord, and he sent you this gift – a little honey and some nuts and spices and myrrh."

They ate and drank together and the brothers planned to leave early next morning. Meanwhile they had their sacks filled with corn at the great store-house, and paid their money as before.

"Put the money back in the sacks," Joseph told his steward secretly, "and put my silver cup in the sack of the youngest brother."

As soon as it was light next day the brothers loaded their donkeys and set off for home. They had not gone far from the city when they were overtaken by the steward himself.

"My lord has sent me," he explained. "He says, why have you repaid his kindness with evil? Why have you stolen his silver cup?" The brothers heard him in amazement, but they willingly let him open their sacks one by one to look for it. He began with the sack of the eldest brother and ended with the sack of Benjamin, and there in Benjamin's sack was the silver cup.

Sadly and slowly they returned to the city and bowed down before Joseph, protesting their innocence.

"You may all go," said Joseph, "except the man who had the cup. He shall stay here and be my servant." Then Judah spoke for all the brothers and begged Joseph to let Benjamin go with them.

"Let me stay and be your servant instead of him, for if he does not come with us our father will die of grief."

Then Joseph could not keep up the pretence any longer and he wept and said,

"I am Joseph your brother, whom you sold into Egypt. Come near to me. Do not grieve and be angry with yourselves, for though it was an evil thing to do, good has come of it, for I have been able to save the lives of all those people who would have died in the famine." His brothers gathered round him, nervous, ashamed, relieved, and he embraced them each in turn.

· · · · · ·

At home in Canaan, Jacob, the father, waited for them. He was full of anxiety. Would the lord of Egypt allow them to return with corn for their families? Would he let Simeon accompany them? Would Benjamin, his favourite son, come back safely? He thought of Joseph, as he often did even now. If he had lived he would be a man of about thirty by this time and a comfort in his father's old age. But Joseph had been dead all these years and Jacob still mourned for him.

Just then he saw a cloud of dust on the road, a long way off. He shaded his eyes against the sun. He saw a confused group of people and donkeys. His sons were returning. Jacob's eyes were dim, and he was puzzled as he peered into the distance. There seemed such a lot of animals and men. Then as they came nearer, he saw that there were many donkeys and that there were wagons too.

"Benjamin! Simeon!" he cried in relief. "Oh my sons, what have you here?"

"Father," they said. "Joseph is still alive and he is governor over all the land of Egypt."

"No," murmured the old man. "That I cannot believe."

"It is true, Father, and the King of Egypt has sent these wagons so that we and all our families may travel to Egypt, with all our household goods, and such of our flocks and herds that still live. He will give land and houses to us so that we shall be near to Joseph. The land will be for us and our children and our children's children."

Then Jacob said,

"It is enough. Joseph my son is still alive. We will go to him."

King of Jazz

It was carnival time in the American city of New Orleans. People had gathered in great surging crowds to watch the procession of Mardi Gras. New Orleans was a huge sea-port at the mouth of the Mississippi River and the inhabitants were descended from people of every country in Europe, particularly Italy and France. There was also a very large population of black people with roots somewhere in Africa.

At the front of the crowd on the edge of the street stood a little boy called Louis. He was very black, with a big, wide, smiling mouth, so wide that he was given the nickname of Satchel Mouth, or Satchmo for short. He wore an odd assortment of bright rags and tatters for the carnival. Most of his friends and neighbours were dressed up in something different from usual. His mother was somewhere in the crowd, in gorgeous silks and satins, and his father was dressed in a monkey suit with marbles in the tip of the tail.

"It's coming!" said Louis eagerly to a friend. "The first band is coming!" A man with a large bass drum led the way, beating a steady rhythm. Others followed, playing horns, cornets, tambourines, bugles. Many of the people who lined the streets were already swaying and swinging to the tune and stamping their feet to the beat of the drum.

Behind the band came horse-drawn floats bearing all kinds of model scenes and people in fancy dress. Many ordinary citizens followed, wearing animal masks or grotesque heads. Scarcely before the first band was out of earshot another came along, and another and another. Then the cry went up,

"The King of the Zulus! The King of the Zulus!" There seemed no good reason for calling him King of the Zulus, as it was unlikely that anyone in New Orleans was actually a Zulu. However, he was the most important person in the whole parade and he was chosen every year from among people who had done something important or helpful in the city. It was a very great honour to be King of the Zulus.

He was dressed in a gown of crimson velvet with golden frills at the neck. He had broad white rings painted round his eyes and mouth. He wore a long black wig and a crown of gold that gleamed in the sun. He was enthroned on a decorated float, which bore him slowly past the waiting crowds. Little Louis gazed at him in awe.

"I wish I could be King of the Zulus," he murmured.

"You might be one day," remarked a woman behind him. Louis smiled his big satchel mouth grin.

"I shouldn't think so," he said.

. . . . . .

Louis lived in one of the worst slums of New Orleans – poor, squalid, sordid. He was surrounded from the beginning of his life by brawling and crime and poverty.

"You might *see* bad things," his mother would tell him, "but there's no need to *do* bad things yourself."

Life was never easy. Sometimes Louis lived with his mother, or his mother and stepfather. Sometimes he lived with his own father and his father's new wife. Sometimes he lived with his grandmother. From the age of seven he did all sorts of jobs to bring in a little money. He sold newspapers. He worked for a junk man. He loaded buckets of coal and carried them round to sell. Yet in spite of everything he was a good-tempered, happy boy, bubbling over with the joy of life. As for New Orleans, it was his birthplace and his home, and he loved it.

His part of the city was a noisy place, filled not only with the strident sounds of ordinary living, but also with music. Many Africans, a few generations back, had brought their own feeling for rhythm and melody with them and it had been passed down to their descendants. New Orleans was often regarded as the home of jazz and it had numerous small bands that marched and played on every possible occasion – funerals, weddings, parties, celebrations. If these bands were booked to play inside a building they would stand outside and play a few tunes first. Groups of children, Louis among them, would stand and listen, stamping their feet, swinging their hips, clapping their hands or dancing.

Then there was church music. The hymn tunes were full of rhythm and joy. Tambourines would often accompany them and the congregations would clap their hands as they sang. Even the sermons were rhythmic and joyful. The preacher would intone a phrase or a sentence and the congregation would repeat it or answer it so that the sermon followed a sort of pattern of sound – from preacher, congregation, preacher, congregation.

When Louis was eleven he formed a quartet with three other boys and they sometimes went round the streets singing and collecting money in a hat. Their voices were surprisingly sweet for rough, tough little urchins, and Louis was delighted when he could run home with his share of the money they received. Up till that time, life was happy enough, but when Louis was twelve years old things changed.

It was New Year's Eve. It was an excuse for noise and celebration and rowdiness on the streets. It was also an excuse for drinking and thieving and brawling, so that the police were particularly watchful and alert. Louis and his friends wanted to celebrate too. They sang. They shouted. They made a noise. Louis surprised and delighted them by firing a rusty pistol into the air with an ear-splitting bang, bang, bang.

"Oh, that's good, Satchmo."

"Where did you get it?"

"Is it loaded?"

'No, they're blanks. I found it in an old trunk of my stepfather's."

"Have you got any more cartridges?"

"Yes." Louis pulled out some more from his pockets, and loaded the pistol again.

"Bang! Bang!"

"Oh it's good, Satchmo. It's good!"

But the pleasure and excitement suddenly faded, as Louis felt a heavy hand on his shoulder. It was the hand of a policeman.

"What's your name?" he demanded, putting the pistol into his own pocket.

"Louis Armstrong."

"You know it's against the law to carry firearms."

"No ... yes. It – it was just for New Year's Eve."

"Where do you live?"

"Jane Alley."

"You'll be hearing more about this."

Louis sighed and his heart sank. He had only been celebrating, thoughtlessly and innocently. Yes, he knew it was against the law to carry a pistol, let alone fire one. He just hadn't thought. It was a very bad start to a new year.

After that came an appearance at a juvenile court, and a sentence of one and a half years in the "Coloured Waifs' Home for Boys". Louis felt that the end of his world had come and for one of the few times in his life he cried and cried and cried.

. . . . .

Discipline was strict in the Waifs' Home, but life was not unpleasant and after a few weeks of homesickness Louis settled down and became his usual cheerful self. He behaved well. He obeyed orders. He was polite and helpful and friendly. His good behaviour was noticed, and he was rewarded by being allowed to play the tambourine and then the drum in the Home's band. After that Professor Davis, the warden, taught him to play the horn and bugle, then the cornet, and finally the trumpet. To Louis, this was sheer joy. He had a wonderful sense of rhythm and played unusually powerful and pure notes. He learned so quickly that he was very soon made leader of the brass band.

Sometimes, with a member of the staff on the big bass drum, the Waifs' Band would march round the streets, giving a performance. One day Professor Davis was leading the way and he took the band to the district where Louis himself belonged. He was quickly recognised.

"There's little Louis!" "There's Satchmo!"
"Cheers for Satch!"
"Here Louis," said one of his old neighbours. "Lend me your hat." He grabbed the band cap from Louis's head and passed it round among his friends and acquaintances. In a few moments he gave it back to Louis, half-full of jingling coins.

"Thanks a lot," said Louis with his well-known grin. He had never seen so much money before and proudly he passed the hat over to Professor Davis. When the boys returned to the Home afterwards, Professor Davis counted the money and found that there was enough to buy much-needed new instruments for the whole band!

The time in the Waifs' Home passed quickly, and when Louis was released after his eighteen months he could read music and he could play marches and melodies on the trumpet with astonishing skill and power. He remembered how he had cried when he had entered the Home. He had thought then that it was the end of the world, but he realised now that it had been only the beginning.

He returned to his mother in the old, squalid slum district. It was good to be back among his friends. It was good to be free once more to stand with them outside the taverns and dance halls, clapping his hands and swinging his hips to the street bands. It was good to earn some money again, though the jobs he did were often far from pleasant – collecting scrap, unloading banana boats, delivering coal, selling papers.

He had no instrument of his own, but he had plenty of opportunity to listen to other people's tunes – the music that was spreading through America under the names of jazz, ragtime and blues. Better still, he was often called upon to take the places of bandsmen who fell sick. Band leaders finding themselves without a trumpeter would say to any handy small boy,

"Go and fetch Louis Armstrong."

"Run and get Satchmo."

"Ask little Louis to come and play."

So he played in small bands in bars where sailors and tourists gathered, and he played in big bands that performed at weddings or celebrations or parades. Everyone in New Orleans soon knew his amazing, clear trumpet notes and his original variations on old and new melodies.

One of his earlier "grown up" jobs was on the river boats that paddled up the Mississippi and the Missouri. Many of them hired bands from New Orleans to entertain the passengers. Louis quickly became extremely popular with his audiences and soon he settled with a band in Chicago for a while. Everyone loved him. He had a warm, glowing personality, and he now became known as a soloist as well as a member of a band. When he played he forgot everything but his trumpet, and if he did think about anything else it was just about happy times. It was said that no one else had ever drawn so much power from a trumpet as Louis did. His throbbing trills, his deep, deep booms and his long, high piercing notes thrilled the people who listened – and soon people were listening not only in America but in Europe, Canada, Australia, India, Japan. Wherever he went he spread good humour and happiness, and with the huge sums of money he earned he spread even more happiness.

. . . . . .

It was carnival time in New Orleans. People had gathered in great surging crowds to watch the procession of Mardi Gras. Tambourines, horns, cornets, bugles, banjos filled the air with a clash of sound; and drums beat out a loud, booming rhythm. Behind the band came gaily trimmed floats on lorries and a horde of human carnival figures. Scarcely before the first band was out of earshot, another came along, and another, and another. Then the cry went up,

"The King of the Zulus! The King of the Zulus!" What an honour to be King of the Zulus! The great man was dressed in a gown of crimson velvet with golden frills at the neck. He had broad white rings painted round his eyes and mouth. He wore a long, black wig and a crown of gold that gleamed in the sun. He was enthroned on a decorated float which bore him slowly past the waiting crowds. He smiled at the people – a great, wide grin of happiness. A roar of delight and pride rose from the crowd. It echoed from street to street and building to building. It echoed down to the wide brown Mississippi River itself.

"Satchmo! It's Satchmo!"

"It's Louis! It's Louis!"

"Satch! Satch!"

"It's Satchmo, King of the Zulus, King of the Trumpet, King of Jazz!"

Bits and Pieces

King Christian III of Holland did not like the way some of his people dressed. They wore elaborate clothes with lots of fancy flaps and unnecessary trimmings. He tried to give an example by wearing plain and sensible clothes himself but fashions seemed to grow only more ridiculous. In despair the King then sent men out into the streets with scissors, and with orders to cut off all foolish, extra bits from the garments of overdressed people.

. . . . . .

Silchester, in England, was built near the site of an old Roman town called Calleva. One day a man was tidying up the rockery in his garden, when he noticed that one of the large stones had interesting markings on it. He scraped away earth and moss and gradually uncovered a carved face. He thought it had probably been carried to his garden at some time from Calleva.

He asked an expert from the local museum to come and see it. It proved to be a head of Jupiter, the Roman god of Thunder, and had been carved in the second century A.D. The strange thing was, that when the head was pulled out from the rockery, a roll of thunder was heard. This was the manner in which Jupiter had always been thought to announce himself.

. . . . . .

Two men were out for a walk when it began to pour with rain. One man carried a rolled umbrella but made no attempt to open it.
First Man: Why don't you open your umbrella?
Second Man: It's no good. It's full of holes.
First Man: Why did you bring it then?
Second Man: I didn't think it would rain.

. . . . . .

Do you know how many hairs you have on your head? It depends on the colour.
  If you are a redhead you have about 90 000.
  If your hair is black you have about 108 000 hairs.
  If your hair is brown you have about 109 000 hairs.
  If you are blonde your total should be about 140 000.
Unlike leaves falling from trees in Autumn, hairs fall out at the rate of about thirty a day. At the same time about thirty new hairs appear daily.

. . . . . .

Written by a traveller in 1611:

"I observed a custom in all those Italian cities and towns through which I passed, that is not used in any other country that I saw in my travels. The Italians do always at their meals use a little fork when they cut their meat. The reason of this their curiosity is, because the Italian cannot by any means endure to have his dish touched with fingers, seeing all men's fingers are not alike clean."

. . . . .

When the famous artist, Renoir, died, art collectors went to the home of his relatives, hoping to buy some of his valuable paintings. They found his canvases in many strange places – stopping holes in the roof of the house, and used for making a rabbit hutch at the end of the garden.

. . . . .

Headline from a local newspaper:

Bus on fire. Passengers alight.

. . . . .

Sir Francis Drake was a famous sea-captain who lived at the time of Elizabeth the First. He took part in many battles, and he saved England from attack by the Spaniards. He was the first Englishman to gaze on the Pacific Ocean, and he was the first to sail round the world. This took him about two and three-quarter years. He died in his own ship, in the West Indies, in the year 1596.

Drake's drum still hangs in the Great Hall of Buckland Abbey, in Devon. It is said that if England needs help, someone has only to beat the drum. Then Drake will awake from his long sleep and come swiftly to his country's aid.

. . . . .

Customer in café: Waiter, will my pancakes be long?
Waiter: No madam, they'll be round.

Fire and Ice

Something disturbed Helga in the middle of the night. What was it? A sort of thudding sound. Was it her little sister Sonja shaking her cot in the same room? Or was it Janni the pony stamping in the lean-to shed at the side of the house? Helga sat up, wide awake. It wasn't only the noise. There was a strange feeling in the air, an eerie, uncanny sensation. She dangled her feet over the side of the bed, and felt for her slippers. She could not find them, so she padded barefoot across the floor to take a peep at three-year-old Sonja. The cot was not there. Puzzled and a little alarmed, she pressed the electric light switch. There was no light.

"Bother! the bulb's gone," she thought.

As her eyes became accustomed to the darkness, she could make out the shadowy shape of the cot at the other side of the room. How had it managed to get there? Surely little Sonja could not have jogged it there herself.

She went to the window, stumbling and almost falling on the way as if the house were rocking. She looked out at the snow that had been lying deep for many days. The pony's door was closed, but he seemed to be stamping about restlessly. Helga loved the pony with all her heart. Perhaps he wanted to get out. From time to time she had an argument with Father about him.

"Icelandic ponies don't need to have stables," Father would say. "They're tough and strong and can fend for themselves."

"Yes, but it's a bit cold in the winter, isn't it?"

"You'll make him soft."

"Oh no, Dad. It'll soon be spring, and then I'll let him run free again."

Father, on this January night, was out fishing in the rich fishing grounds beyond Iceland and beyond the small island of Heimaey, where the family lived. Helga gave him a passing thought and shivered for him. Then her attention returned to the noise – not only of Janni's stamping, but of something else, a rumbling sound that seemed both near and distant.

Then, on the hillside, she noticed a strange thing. A little red river was trickling down through the snow. Red! A red river, fiery red and jewel bright, gleaming under an uncanny glow in the sky. For a moment she was frightened because she thought it was a river of blood. Blood? How could it be blood? The next moment there was a mighty roar; and a great surge of flame and glowing rock leaped out of the snow, and pierced the sky.

"It's a volcano erupting!" thought Helga. There

had been many volcanoes on Iceland in times past, but this one on Heimaey had been extinct for five thousand years! Five thousand years! But now it was rumbling and roaring, tearing the island apart and spurting up in a mighty fountain of flame and lava and ash.

Quickly Helga ran to the next room, shaking and calling her mother.

"Mother, Mother, wake up. There's an eruption." Then she went to her brother's room.

"Stefan, Stefan, wake up, wake up."

They all knew what to do. Grab a blanket and hurry down to the harbour in the hope of escaping to the mainland. They put on coats and shoes and pulled blankets off their beds. Mother lifted up the still-sleeping Sonja, and without another word they rushed out of the house and stumbled down the stony path towards the harbour. At one point in the journey, Helga missed Stefan and wondered where he was.

"He's probably in front," she thought.

Very soon Mother, Helga and Sonja had joined a group of people at the harbour. They were nearly all in their night clothes and wrapped up in coats or blankets, swarming anxiously on to a boat that had been just about to start off on its fishing trip. Some of the people carried small children. One or two held cats. One had a canary in a cage, and another clutched a yelping dog.

"Where's Stefan?" asked Mother in a desperate voice.

"He's coming." There he was, bringing Janni the pony.

"Oh Stefan, you are good!" cried Helga, a little ashamed that she hadn't brought the pony herself, but overjoyed and relieved to see him. She clutched Janni's white, shaggy mane, and Stefan grinned and pulled his slipping blanket up round his shoulders.

The skipper of the boat helped Mother and Sonja aboard, then Stefan; but at Helga and Janni he paused.

"Sorry my dear," he said. "I can't take the pony." Helga's cheeks went pink with horror.

"But – but," she stammered.

"Sorry," he said again. "People first. It's only fair, isn't it? There's sure to be a rescue ship for animals later."

Helga stood, unhappy and irresolute, blocking the gangway.

"Go on," someone said to her impatiently, with a nervous eye on the stream of fire and lava thrusting itself through the crust of the earth.

"Helga, you'll have to leave him," said Mother. "He'll take up too much room on the boat." A woman was trying to pass two toddlers up to a fisherman. Helga was in the way, terribly in the way.

"Janni," called Stefan suddenly, "run away. Run." Helga let go of the pony's mane, and Janni turned and trotted obediently away.

"Don't worry," said a woman kindly, as Helga stumbled blindly and tearfully on to the boat. "All the animals will be rescued tomorrow, I expect. Think of all the sheep and cows and cats and dogs, and all the ponies like yours. They won't be left to die, I'm sure."

"I suppose I ought to have left him at home," said

Stefan sadly, as Helga rejoined the family.

"Well," replied Mother, "I think it's a good thing that you set him free. He'll have more chance of keeping himself safe somewhere and finding something to eat."

Helga felt very sad and wondered if she would ever see Janni again, but she stood with everyone else facing the island that had always been her home, and watching a cloud of fire in the sky and a stream of boiling lava running down the hillside. No one panicked or complained, though some were watching their own houses going up in flames and others could see that theirs would be buried in volcanic ash.

Other boats were leaving and arriving now, as fishermen returned from the fishing grounds and filled up at once with passengers.

"That's Dad's boat," declared Stefan, pointing to a nearby shadow approaching Heimaey. "I'm sure it is."

"I hope so," said Mother. "He will take people to the mainland, no doubt."

More and more people were leaving their homes now; and aeroplanes and helicopters were helping with the evacuation. The fishing boat bore the family further and further out to sea, rocking violently. Their last glimpse of Heimaey was of a house silhouetted against a wall of flame and sliding sideways into destruction, with a gigantic cloud of glowing fire in the sky above.

"Hell must look like that," observed Stefan cheerfully. Then the boat swung round and the island was lost to sight.

. . . . .

In about four hours, most of the inhabitants (over five thousand of them) had been taken safely away from the island. Only two hundred rescue workers remained, apart from a few brave, devoted old people who said they had been born on Heimaey and would die there. The rescued families were taken into the homes of friends and relatives and kind strangers in and around the city of Reykjavik on the mainland. Helga found herself in a comfortable house near the harbour, where a girl of similar age lent her some clothes and seemed delighted to have her company. Stefan stayed there too, but Mother and Sonja were given hospitality in another house close by.

The eruption had taken place on the night of January the twenty-third. Two days later, a rescue plan was organised for the animals. Stefan heard the news as the first of the "Noah's Ark" rescue boats was approaching land. He rushed into the house calling,

"Helga, Helga, the animals will soon be here. Come and look for Janni." Helga glanced up with relief and hope. Then turning to Erna, her new friend, she asked anxiously,

"Where shall we keep my pony?"

"It'll be arranged for you," Erna assured her. "Farmers around the city have offered to care for all animals free of charge. I'm afraid you'll be separated for a while though."

"Oh I won't mind that, as long as I know Janni's safe. Will you come with us to see him land?"

Soon the three children stood with other Heimaey people watching a freighter unloading a mixed collection of animals. Cats and dogs were welcomed with cries of delight by their owners. Crates of squawking hens were placed on the quayside. Sheep were led away by waiting farmers and their dogs. Icelandic ponies stepped ashore. These strong little horses, with bright eyes and flowing manes, were of various colours. Some were black, some were brown, some were grey or white, and some were a mixture of shades.

Helga could hardly wait. Janni was a beautiful shaggy white, with touches of grey about him. She scanned each animal eagerly as it came ashore. Some were claimed at once. Others were led away to waiting horse boxes. Helga looked and waited. Not Janni, not Janni, not Janni yet. She became impatient. She became anxious. She became frantic with worry.

"He's not there! He's not there!" she cried.

"Wait a minute," said Stefan calmly. "There are still some more to come." There was a pause of several minutes. Then another lot were led ashore. Brown ponies, black ponies, grey ponies, white ponies, but not Janni. Helga was in tears now.

"There's another boat expected in half an hour," remarked a sailor, seeing her distress. "Another freighter, *Ocean Star*."

Helga, Stefan and Erna waited. They waited, gazing across the water at the smoke darkening the sky sixteen kilometres away, above Heimaey. More than half an hour passed. *Ocean Star* arrived. It drew into harbour. More sheep were unloaded and a few goats, some cows and a few more horses. A black Icelandic pony came, and one with a mottled coat, three little donkeys and five more ponies. A black pony, a brown one, two white ones and a grey, but not Janni. Janni was still on Heimaey. Perhaps he had been killed by falling, boiling rock.

"There may be some more boats tomorrow," said Erna, trying to comfort Helga. There were. There were boats bringing radios and refrigerators and cupboards and cabinets and cars. There were boats bringing tables and television sets and beds and chairs and blankets and fishing equipment and machinery and stocks of dried fish. There were numerous boxes labelled with the names of those who owned the contents. There were all sorts of ordinary possessions. There were even some more animals, but not Janni. Janni had not come.

. . . . . .

Heimaey was a small island, only 4.8 kilometres by 3 kilometres, with only thirty-two kilometres of road. Its main industry was highly successful fishing, and there were modern and very efficient fish-processing factories. There were eleven hundred houses, and the standard of living was high. When the volcano erupted it was thought that the island would have to be abandoned and left to the destructive forces of nature. Many houses were buried beneath lava and volcanic ash. Others were set on fire by burning rocks that fell through the roofs. Others simply caved in and disappeared. Some, according to the changes in wind direction, were almost unharmed, even if liberally sprayed with blowing dust. A river of molten lava flowed down to the sea and along the coast towards the harbour. The harbour was Heimaey's greatest asset and it seemed as if it might become narrowed and ruined.

If Heimaey were going to be destroyed, everything possible must be saved; and teams of rescuers went from house to house packing and labelling and moving out all that could be salvaged. Telephone lines, of course, were out of action but news came through to the mainland from day to day with the boats.

– Heimaey would be unusable for years to come. It would have to be left to the puffins and the waves.

– Heimaey would *not* be abandoned. Many houses could be repaired and saved. Hundreds of people were determined to go back and live there as soon as it was safe to do so.

– Workers were trying to save the harbour and the town by directing a constant stream of sea water on to the lava flow, to cool and divert it.

– Many of the houses were so deeply buried in black ash that you could walk over the roof tops and touch the chimneys.

A day or two later, as Helga and Stefan were walking back with Erna to her home, after watching the unloading of the last boat of the day, they heard hurrying footsteps behind them.

"Oh, it's Axel," said Stefan. "Hullo, Axel." He was a young man who worked in the library at home.

"I've a letter for your mother," he said. "I think it's from your father."

"Oh good," said Stefan.

"How is he?" asked Helga.

"Well I haven't seen him at all. I was given the letter with a handful of others for different people. Bit of a job to find them all."

"What's it like at home?"

"Very strange and eerie. Makes you feel you're walking on the moon. We'll be back though, in a few months. We'll all be back. You'll see."

"When the old volcano stops breathing fire," remarked Stefan.

"It isn't the old volcano actually. People say it's her daughter a few kilometres along. Well, I've only twenty-four hours ashore, so I must hurry. My job is scraping tonnes of ashes from rooftops at present. – Oh, your letter." He pulled a crumpled envelope from his pocket.

"Oh dear. It's rather wet, I'm afraid. I had a little

trouble with a shower of spray on the way over. Sorry about that."

"Never mind. We'll soon dry it. Thanks for bringing it, Axel." It was indeed wet – not merely wet, but sodden.

The children took it into the house where Mother was living. Little Sonja nestled up to Helga.

"Why don't you stay with us?" she asked. Mother and Stefan unfolded the letter and spread it out carefully on a tea towel.

"Oh, the ink's run," wailed Mother. "Half the writing's obliterated."

"It's terribly smudgy," said Helga. "Read it out to us, Mother."

Mother read slowly, picking out the readable bits and making wild guesses at the unreadable bits.

"We're lucky," Father had written. "Our house is hardly damaged – just some ashes to clear away at one end. I started on the job on the second day, and – " The rest of the page was so wet that it was almost falling apart and was quite impossible to read. Then there was a mention of a man called Sven Kristianson, who lived outside Reykjavik.

"Do you know him, Mum?" asked Helga.

"No. I've never heard of him."

"What does Dad say about him?"

"I don't know. I can't read it."

"Go on, go on," said Stefan impatiently. The last two sentences were quite clear,

"The eruption is still going strong, like a firework display. We are working to try and save the harbour." – then, "Love to you all."

"Oh dear," sighed Helga. "I wonder what the middle part says."

"Never mind," said Mother. "It's wonderful to hear that the house is still standing."

"Axel said we'll all be going back to Heimaey in a month or two," remarked Stefan.

"Yes. That's what a lot of people are hoping," said Mother. "It depends partly on the way the wind blows."

"And where the lava stream flows."

Mother and Stefan were filled with relief and hope,

but Helga thought continually of Janni. She had hoped that Father would have said something about him in his letter. He probably had no idea of course, that the pony was running loose. Janni might have been very frightened and run to hide in a cavern somewhere, and be slowly starving to death. Helga knew it was most unlikely that she would ever see him again.

. . . . . .

It was now three weeks since the beginning of the eruption. Helga and Stefan had started school in the city with Erna, and life had fallen into a more regular routine. Stefan fitted happily enough into the new school, but Helga found it difficult to concentrate on lessons.

One day after school she went to see Mother and Sonja, as she always did. There was a car outside the house and a stranger in the living room.

"Helga," said Mother, "this is Sven Kristianson." Helga shook hands and wondered where she had heard the name before. He was a tall, friendly man, and he looked down at her and said,

"When are you coming to see your pony?"

"My pony?" murmured Helga.

"Yes. His name's Janni, isn't it?"

"Oh yes. Is he safe then? Do you know where he is?"

Now her words tumbled out in excitement, and she suddenly remembered that Sven Kristianson was the man Father had mentioned in his letter. He laughed at her bewilderment and began to explain.

"Yes, he's safe. He's been on my farm for nearly three weeks. I have a flock of Heimaey sheep there too. They came by air, but your pony came by boat. Apparently when your father cleared the ashes off your house, he found the pony trapped in its stable. It was quite unhurt and hadn't even been affected by fumes because there was a rack of thick straw above its head. A friend of your father's brought Janni over to me. I thought you knew about it. Why don't you all get in my car and come out to the farm to see him?"

"Oh yes please," agreed Helga in delight, adding, "And here's Stefan too. He's just in time."

Mother, Helga, Stefan and Sonja crowded into the car, and in a short time they had been driven out into the country. The day was very grey, and though there were stretches of grass, there was still a lot of snow about.

"There he is!" shouted Stefan. "There's Janni." There he was, white with touches of grey, sturdy and strong, with his shaggy mane hanging half over his eyes. Sven Kristianson stopped the car and Helga scrambled out, followed by the rest of the family.

"Janni, Janni," she murmured, and he rubbed his head against her. She ran her fingers through his damp hair and pressed her face close to him so that no one should see that she was crying with relief and happiness.

. . . .

In early July, scientists announced that the eruption was over. Five hundred houses had been damaged and a fish-processing plant destroyed. The hands of the clock in the main street had stuck at two o'clock when vibrations had stopped it on the night of January the twenty-third. Far from being ruined, the harbour had actually been improved by a wall of lava that sheltered and protected it from storms. Aircraft flew over the island, sowing grass seed. Building started on the first of the new houses to be erected. People began to return to their homes. Life was beginning again on Heimaey.

The Lost Woman of San Nicolas

There are several stories about people who have been marooned on lonely islands for months or even years, but perhaps the saddest of the stories is that of the Lost Woman of San Nicolas. She was stranded, not in any place strange to her, but on the very island that had always been her home.

The island was one of a group off the coast near Los Angeles. It was stormy and windswept, with no trees and very little water. Nevertheless, a tribe of Indians lived there happily enough until they were attacked by a shipload of marauders, hunting sea otters that bred around the beaches. In the battle that followed, nearly two-thirds of the San Nicolas men were killed, and half of those that were left were too old to fight or hunt.

After that, life became even harder and harsher than it had been before, and the women had to take over much of the men's work. They had to trap sea birds and catch fish and wade out into the rock pools to harvest kelp and shellfish. When a year or two had passed, it was decided that the island should be evacuated and that all its remaining inhabitants should be taken to a more hospitable place to live. For this purpose, in the year 1835, a sailing ship dropped anchor beyond the breakers, and white men from the crew came ashore in rowing boats to pick up the people. The Indians could not understand the white men's language, but they realised that they were urging them to hurry because the wind was rising and a storm seemed to be imminent.

Scrambling on to one of the boats, excited about the new life ahead and sad at leaving the old life behind, was a girl of twelve. She was an orphan, and she had a lively little brother of six who had run down to the beach in front of her and who was now, she believed, in the first of the rowing boats. Someone said he had seen the little boy clambering aboard. This was true, but in the hurry and confusion, no one had noticed that he had jumped out again and had run back home for something he had meant to take with him.

Only when the girl had searched the crowded deck of the sailing ship did she begin to worry. The ship was tossing wildly and it was difficult to walk steadily on it.

"Have you seen my little brother? Where's my little brother?" she asked.

"I saw him on the first boat," said someone.

"He may be exploring down below the deck," said someone else. Then suddenly, someone pointed towards the shore. There in the distance was the small boy running along the cliff towards the beach path.

"Oh please let me go back for him," the girl begged the captain. She could not understand his reply, but she knew he was refusing. The ship had already spread its sails. It was already moving. Even now it was in danger. The storm would break upon it at any moment. All these lives were at risk. He would come back in a day or two.

"Oh please, please." The girl was frantic with worry. Friends and neighbours tried to comfort her.

"The captain can't turn back now. It's too stormy," they explained. "He'll come back another day. Your brother will be all right. There's plenty of food in the huts. He can sleep in his own home. It won't be for long."

"Oh, I can't leave him all alone!" She was a brave girl and she was desperate. Before anyone could stop her, she had climbed over the side of the ship and leaped into the stormy water. She was a strong swimmer and had often swum long distances, though never in quite such a stormy sea and never in circumstances like this. The Indians watched her in horror. For a moment they saw her, bobbing on the surface of the water, then disappearing between great waves, then appearing again. Only for a moment they watched her. Then the darkness of the sky and the increasing fury of the sea hid her from sight; and the sailing ship ploughed its way through the storm to a future that no one could possibly guess.

The girl reached the shore in safety. She hugged her frightened little brother and scolded him for causing so much trouble.

"You're very naughty. You shouldn't have run back."

"I didn't know the sailing ship would start so soon. I'm sorry, really I am. What will happen to us now?" He rubbed his eyes and began to cry.

"Never mind. The ship will come back for us in a few days. Don't worry. We'll be all right."

"Do you think the ship will come tomorrow?"

"No, not tomorrow. That would be too soon to expect it."

"The next day?"

"No, I shouldn't think so."

"Do you think it will come the day after that?"

"Perhaps. I don't know. I think the captain will land our people at their new home before he comes back for us."

"Where are we all going to live?"

"On the mainland somewhere, I think."

"I wish the ship would come today."

"Oh well, we must just wait patiently and keep a lookout every day."

The evacuation had taken place so suddenly that the Indians had had no time to prepare for it, and they had been able to take with them only the few things they could carry in their hands. There were, therefore, still some baskets of food in the children's hut – some dried roots and shellfish, and even a fresh fish that a kind friend had caught for them that morning.

The day passed and evening came. The girl and her little brother curled up together on the floor in the usual place, surrounded by the simple, familiar things of their home. The little boy probably slept the deep, untroubled sleep of the very young, but possibly the girl lay awake a long time, listening to the howling of the wind round the hut and the ceaseless, angry pounding of the waves upon the shore. She felt, also, the great emptiness and loneliness of the island now that everyone else had gone away. There was another sound too – the baying of the wild dogs that lived in the caves over the hill. She was well used to their noise and normally took little notice of it, but tonight it frightened her and filled her with an inexplicable sense of foreboding.

. . . . . .

Then two terrible tragedies took place. The ship that was carrying the people of San Nicolas sank in the storm before it reached its destination. The crew and all the Indian passengers were drowned, so there was no one left to remember the two children stranded alone on the island; and no ship ever set forth with the intention of rescuing them.

Somewhere around the same time, the little brother was attacked and killed by the wild dogs. Possibly, with all the other huts empty and food lying unprotected, the dogs had become bolder, or perhaps the little boy, bored and tired of waiting for the ship, had become too adventurous and had run into danger.

Think of the feelings of the twelve-year-old girl now! Grieving for her brother, longing for her people, she waited day after day, week after week for a ship that did not come. She must have been very sad and puzzled. Why didn't the ship come back for her? Surely all her friends and neighbours would not abandon her entirely!

Her life had become one great loneliness, and we can only imagine how she filled the desolate hours. At first she could wander in and out of the deserted huts and thankfully take the food that she found. Then when it was all finished she would have to work hard to provide for herself every day – fishing, trapping sea birds, wading into the sea and wrenching shellfish from the rocks and gathering bundles of kelp. When her clothes wore out she would have to make new ones by sewing bird skins together and trimming them with feathers. Again and again she would stand on the cliffs and watch for a ship. Fighting against the wind, straining her eyes against the sun, she would watch and wait and watch and wait and watch and wait.

Her birthdays came and went. She was no longer twelve. She was thirteen. She was fourteen. She was fifteen. She was growing up all alone. Perhaps the great sadness of the early days gave way eventually to a sort of appreciation of the solitude and to moments of pleasure when there were beautiful sunsets, or when pretty shells were cast up on the shore.

We know that she tamed one of the dogs and made a companion of it, but any other reconstruction of her life can only be guesswork and our own imagination.

We do, however, know a little about the end of the story. For eighteen years the girl, the woman, was alone. Then in the year 1853 a man called Captain George Nidever brought his ship to the island to hunt for otters. He did not find any, but he found instead the woman who has gone down in history as "The Lost Woman of San Nicolas."

The little girl of twelve had become a woman of thirty, and she was taken to the Mission of Santa Barbara, on the Californian coast. There, a priest named Father Gonzales gave her friendship and tried to learn something of her story. There were many Indians in and around the mission. They spoke various languages or dialects, but no one could speak the language of San Nicolas. It was sad to think that after all her years of solitude, the woman of San Nicolas was unable to converse with people when at last she mixed with them again. Only by sign language did she learn from Father Gonzales that the ship carrying the Indians of her tribe had sunk. There was no one, no one left at all. The people, the language had gone.

Some notes written by a man at the mission were discovered as long afterwards as 1978. These made mention of the Lost Woman, and described a dress that she had made of seabird skins sewn neatly together, with holes left for the arms. The hem was trimmed with feathers, all facing the same way – "a beautiful piece of work." There was also a skirt of cormorant feathers that gleamed in the sun. This was sent to Rome, and there perhaps it still remains, a memento of a sad, brave, lonely life.

Very Short Stories

Story 1

Towards the end of the last century, two children were playing on a beach in Western Australia when they saw an albatross floating near the water's edge. It appeared to be half dead, and it had a large fish in its mouth which it was unable to swallow. The children tried to drag it ashore but it was too heavy so they called their father to come and help them.

"Poor thing!" said the father. "It's choking to death. Look! There's a sort of collar round its neck." The three of them managed to pull the bird on to the beach and the father unfastened the collar and released the albatross.

"It's not a real collar," said one of the children. "It's made of tin." It had been roughly cut from an old tin that had once held preserved meat, and some words had been punched on it with a nail.

"It's a message," said the children. It was indeed a message, punched painfully out in French.

"13 castaways on Crozet Islands. Help for the love of God." Then there followed a date, showing that the collar had been put on the bird twelve days before. If the castaways had been hungry then, they must surely be starving by now.

The children's father delivered the message to the governor, who sent a telegram to the admiral in charge of the area. Tragically the admiral delayed, saying that the Crozet Islands came under the Cape of Good Hope. For some reason he was unable to get in touch with the authorities there, so he cabled Paris, and at last a gunboat was sent to the rescue.

Alas! It was too late. When the crew scrambled ashore and searched the desolate islands, there was no one to be found. There was, however, another section of meat tin with a further message punched weakly on it. This one said,

"Gone on raft in search of food."

Nothing more was ever heard of the unfortunate castaways.

Story 2

For a hundred years a large picture hung in a famous English Abbey. It was in rather a dark place, and no one took much notice of it. Then one day it was taken down and put in the vestry, where the choir boys hung their robes. It was propped against the wall, out of the way, and was soon forgotten.

One day a stranger walked into the abbey. He was an art expert and he knew how to clean and restore old paintings. In fact, he had his cleaning things with him. He looked round the abbey and then walked into the vestry. There he saw the picture propped against the wall. He knew at once that it was a famous picture by an Italian artist. He knew it had been painted in Rome, about the year 1550.

He felt very angry to think that the abbey cared so little about such a precious picture. He cleaned one little corner of it so that its colours gleamed brightly as they were meant to do. Then he pinned a note on it, saying,

"You should look after your treasures better than this."

Then the stranger walked quietly away. No one had seen him come, no one saw him leave and no one ever found out who he was. But the people in charge of the abbey read the note and they sent to London for another art expert to come and see the painting. This man assured them that they did indeed possess a picture of great value.

"It is a real treasure," he said. "It was painted by a famous Italian artist, about the year 1550 in Rome." So the people in charge of the abbey sold the picture for a great deal of money, which they badly needed to pay for repairs to the ancient building.

Mad About Bones

Gideon Algernon Mantell was a doctor. He was rather handsome, with dark, curly hair and a thin, sensitive face. He worked in the small city of Lewes, walking to the homes of his local patients or driving a horse and carriage along the green lanes of Sussex to those who lived out in the country. He was a good doctor but he spent a lot of time on a personal hobby which meant rather more to him than the study of medicine. He collected shells and fossils and bones, and he had written a book on the subject, called *The Fossils of the South Downs*, illustrated by his wife, Mary. It was to be published this very year, 1822.

He was particularly interested in the large bones of ancient reptiles. These creatures must once have made their homes in the South Downs area, or else their skeletons had been washed there in a later upheaval of earth. Dr Mantell had found several broken fragments of bone, as well as one or two large segments, and it was his ambition to build up a museum of his own.

One morning in the spring, when he had a country call to make, he said to his wife,

"Why don't you come with me, Mary? It's a beautiful day."

"Yes, I think I will," she replied. So she climbed up

into the carriage and they set off down the road and out into the beauty of the open countryside.

When the doctor reached his patient's house, he knocked at the door, and Mary wandered along in the sunshine. Very soon she came upon a pile of stones, left in readiness for some road repairs. From habit, she glanced down, looking for fossils. She saw broken rocks and lumps of chalky stone, and there among them was something shining. It was partly embedded in a piece of rock. It was not a fossil. Nor was it part of a bone. She stared at it intently and ran her fingers over the exposed surface. It looked like a tooth, a large, unusual tooth, perhaps sixteen or eighteen centimetres long. She moved a few stones from the pile and pulled out the one she wanted. Then she walked back to the carriage and waited impatiently for her husband. After a while he came out of the house.

"Gideon!" she said eagerly, "look at this! It was in a pile of stones at the side of the road."

The doctor looked and his excitement was apparent.

"A tooth!" he exclaimed. "This is something really interesting, Mary. A tooth! And so big! Now what animal would this have belonged to?" They both walked back to the pile of stones, but there appeared to be nothing more of interest in it.

"I'll come out again tomorrow and find out which quarry these came from," said the doctor.

He was a moody man, rather domineering and autocratic, and not at all easy to live with, but for the next few days he was excited, elated, walking on air. This discovery of Mary's was something really important, something new, strange, mysterious. He guessed that the tooth had belonged to some sort of gigantic, extinct reptile. Yet its biting surface was worn in such a way that it must have been used to chew leaves and stems and vegetable matter, which reptiles did not normally eat. What animal had owned the tooth?

There were several stone quarries in the neighbourhood, and when Dr Mantell had found out which one had produced the tooth, he went along and showed it to the quarrymen and chatted to them. They had often found fossils and unusual shells and petrified fish as they daily broke up the rocks for roads but they had never found anything like this.

"Keep a look-out," the doctor asked them. "You may find some more, or perhaps some bones from this same creature."

They agreed to do so, and he visited the quarry again and again. Eventually he or the men found more teeth of the same kind. Now Doctor Mantell was a member of the London Geological Society, so when he went to the next meeting, he took some of the teeth with him and showed them to some of the geologists and famous scientific thinkers of the day.

"What did they say?" asked Mary eagerly that evening, when he returned home. She had expected him to be full of pride and excitement, but he seemed dispirited and indignant.

"They thought they were of no great interest," he replied. "Someone suggested that they belonged to a relative of the wolf-fish, and someone said they must be mammal's teeth. Rubbish! They are neither fish nor mammal! That I know! Only one man agreed with me that they might belong to a hitherto unknown, plant-eating reptile."

Soon afterwards a friend of Doctor Mantell was going to visit Paris, and he agreed to take one of the teeth to a very learned man called Baron Cuvier, who was an expert on fossils and living animals. A week or two later, the friend returned with the tooth and with Baron Cuvier's report on it.

"The upper tooth of a rhinoceros."

Mantell was cast into a state of gloom. Rhinoceros! Baron Cuvier was the greatest authority on the subject, but Mantell was certain that in this case he was wrong. Rhinoceros!

"It certainly is not a rhinoceros," he muttered to his wife.

Some time after this disappointment his depression was lifted by the discovery of some great leg bones in the same quarry. These, too, he sent to Paris, and was informed that they were part of the front leg of a species of hippopotamus. Later, in the same level of rock, one of the quarrymen found a horn, and the experts declared that this was indeed from a rhinoceros.

Wolf-fish, mammal, rhinoceros, hippopotamus! How wrong, how impossible were all these theories! How mistaken were all the experts! Gideon Mantell was sure that the teeth, the bones, the horn all belonged to the same creature, and that creature was a hitherto unknown, long-extinct kind of reptile that fed on vegetation. He was sure. He was certain.

Time passed, a year, two years, and the mystery remained. Dr Mantell then thought of going to the Hunterian Museum at the Royal College of Surgeons. Here, there were hundreds of remains of hundreds of different animals – hundreds of bones and hundreds of teeth. Mantell spent a whole day hunting through them. He found nothing like his precious Sussex teeth and bones at all, but by sheer coincidence there was a young man in the museum that day who appeared interested in the fruitless search.

"What are you looking for?" he asked.

"A tooth like this," replied Mantell, producing his sample.

"Good gracious!" exclaimed the young man, taking

it with excited, loving care. "This *is* a coincidence! Look at this!" He opened a box, and showed Mantell the carefully packed skeleton of a Central American lizard, an iguana.

"I've been working on iguanas for months," he explained. "I'd recognise any part of them with my eyes shut. Look at these teeth. Mine are small and yours are very big, but they are the same shape, aren't they? You must have found a giant, extinct iguana!"

Here was the answer to the puzzle. Here was the answer to the experts. The teeth, bones and horn from Sussex belonged to a huge, extinct, previously unknown reptile of the iguana type. By this time three years had passed since Mary Mantell had found the tooth beside the road, but now the iguana-type owner of it was recognised and accepted by the experts.

It was given a name – Iguanodon, meaning "iguana tooth", and it opened up a vision of a prehistoric world, inhabited unbelievably by the giant creatures we now call dinosaurs. The iguanodon was one of them.

. . . . . .

There were times when Mrs Mary Mantell must have wished fervently that she had never found the famous tooth. Gideon continued with his medical practice. He would have liked to have given it up, but he could not afford to do so, especially as he now had four young children to support. He continued also with his collection of fossils and bones. Some he discovered and dug out of the earth himself. Others he bought and some he procured by a method of exchange with other enthusiasts. The collection was soon large enough to fill the drawing-room and be regarded as a museum, so it was opened to the public twice a month. As he was a doctor he could not charge for admission, though he would have liked the money. Many of the people who came to see it were scientists who had a real interest in it, but others came merely out of curiosity to see the inside of the fine house on Lewes High Street.

Gideon became less interested in his medical work and more interested in his collection. It became the most important thing in his life. Bones filled his thoughts, his days, his dreams. He was mad about bones. He cared more about them than he did about his patients, and more, Mary realised sadly, than he did about his wife.

The iguanodon tooth became part of history, but the home life of the Mantell family did not. We can only guess at the frustrations and resentments that Mary must have felt. Not only were bones beginning to creep into one part of the house after another, but she was continually annoyed and disturbed by people who expected to view the museum on any day they fancied.

Then there were the children. They must have been taught not to scamper about indoors in case they shook and damaged Father's bones. They must have been taught also that he needed peace and quiet for his studies and his correspondence and his writing and the preparation of the lectures he often gave. All the same, they grew up to be interested in geology and zoology themselves, but Mary must have become more bitter and unhappy over the years.

When the youngest child was six years old, it became obvious that the house in Lewes was too small for the family (or rather, for the family *and* the bones) so the Mantells moved to Brighton, to a new medical practice and a bigger house. The finest room in the new house was the drawing-room, so of course that was taken over at once for the collection of bones and fossils – along with any other room that might be regarded as "spare."

Mary and the children settled down at Brighton. Gideon procured more and more specimens. As far as the family was concerned, the big house seemed to become smaller and smaller. Then, a year after the move, a man called Mr Bensted found part of another iguanodon skeleton in a quarry that he owned in Maidstone, Kent. There was one very large piece of bone and there were many smaller pieces that had been separated and broken by blasting. There were bones from back legs and bones from front legs. There were bones from feet and broken bits of ribs. There were vertebrae from an incredibly long spine, and there was part of a tooth.

Mr Bensted collected every scrap that he could find. He chipped them from the rock in which most were embedded. He stuck some of them together and he arranged the whole collection in its right pattern. It was as if he were doing a huge jigsaw puzzle, and when it was as complete as he could make it, it showed clearly the framework of an unbelievably large creature – a giant from a past age – an iguanodon.

When news of this reached Brighton, Mary and the older children groaned. Father would *have* to buy it.

They knew he would *have* to buy it. And where would it go? Probably the children were already sharing bedrooms. Probably almost all the ground floor rooms were full of bones. Gideon was thrilled and excited. He arranged to call on Mr Bensted at Maidstone. He planned to make an offer for the iguanodon.

"Gideon, don't buy it. Don't bring any more bones into the house. It's nearly full of them now. The children are being crowded out of their own home. Please, please stop before it is too late." Mary must have begged and pleaded, but it was no good. Gideon was determined to possess the skeleton. So, of course, a month or two later he was on his hands and knees (probably in the dining room) laying out the long-dead iguanodon. From nose to tail-tip it stretched the whole length of the floor and (probably) the family, in future, had to eat in the kitchen. It is known that within little more than a year after the move to Brighton, Gideon's bones were filling nearly the whole house. They dominated it. They owned it. They possessed it. The house was a family home no longer. It was a museum.

Four years after that, when the youngest child was eleven and the others were almost grown up, Mrs Mary Mantell left Gideon, never to return. She had borne enough. In a letter that he wrote to a friend, the doctor said sadly,

"There was a time when my poor wife felt deep interest in my pursuits, and was proud of my success, but of late years that feeling had passed away, and she was annoyed rather than gratified by my devotion to science." Beneath his autocratic rule of his family, Gideon was kind and well-meaning but he was thoughtless and selfish too, and his bones and fossils blinded him to the rights and feelings of Mary and the children.

. . . . . .

There is a little more to the story of the iguanodon. Geologists and zoologists decided that it rested its huge body on four legs, though the front ones were obviously considerably shorter than the back ones. They decided too, that the horn came from the tip of its nose. These suppositions were wrong, but they were believed for many years. It was then considered that the iguanodon had more likely walked on its hind legs (reaching a height of 4.3 metres) and that the horn was an offensive and defensive weapon attached to the thumb.

While the earlier opinions were still held, the famous Crystal Palace was built to house the Great Exhibition of 1851, and when the exhibition was over, the palace was moved to Sydenham, outside London. Here, among many other delights, a group of life-sized figures of prehistoric animals was placed in a natural, swamp-like setting. The animals were constructed by a man called Waterhouse Hawkins, and among them was the iguanodon. When it was partly built, a dinner was held in its body for twenty well-known scientists and other men of importance. Then Waterhouse Hawkins continued with its re-creation. He used,

600 bricks

900 plain tiles

650 small half-round drain tiles

  38 casks of cement

90 casks of broken stone

30 metres of iron hooping

6 metres of cube-shaped bar.

In 1854 Queen Victoria opened the Crystal Palace to the public again in its new surroundings. Gideon Mantell, alas, was not able to view his beloved iguanodon in its full reconstructed glory, as he had died two years earlier.

Today it may still be seen in the Crystal Palace grounds; and Mary Mantell's iguanodon tooth is now on view in the Natural History Museum in London. As for the iguanodon skeleton that Mantell purchased from Mr Bensted at Maidstone, it is now remembered in the city coat of arms, where it stands, plump and proud as in life.

Lion of Two Worlds

Mrs Adamson was wondering when her husband, George, would return. It might be today or tomorrow or the next day, or even later. He was the senior game warden of a huge area in Kenya. He had gone away now with two or three other men in search of a man-eating lion that had killed a tribesman in some distant hills.

Although she was alone, Joy Adamson was never lonely. There was always something to watch. There might be a group of giraffes among the thorn bushes in the distance, or a curious elephant coming near to the house. There were waterbuck and antelope passing by, and usually a crowd of baboons barking from the rocks. There was the odd rhino or a herd of gazelles, or a slow tortoise in view. Mongooses came out in the early evening to feed on berries and grubs. There were bush babies, squirrels and bat-eared foxes.

This morning Joy was finishing some paintings she had done of Africans when suddenly she heard the roar and rattle of a Land Rover. George was back. She had not expected him so soon.

"Joy!" he shouted. "Come quickly! Come quickly!" She ran out, wondering what the hurry was.

"Look," he said, pointing to the back of the Land

Rover. She looked. She saw three tiny lion cubs curled up like fluffy balls. They were no more than a few weeks old, and they mewed piteously like worried kittens.

"Oh! Aren't they sweet?" cried Joy, and she picked them up and cuddled them and tried to comfort them. She was enchanted with them, but George was obviously most unhappy.

"I wouldn't have had it happen for anything," he said. "A lioness charged us. We had to shoot her to save ourselves. Poor thing! She was only protecting her babies. We found them a little later. I had to bring them home, otherwise they would have died."

"Of course," murmured Joy. "Poor little things. They are very young. Their eyes are not properly open yet."

Three little lion cubs! What was to be done with them? That was a question that George and Joy did not even try to answer at present. They simply got on with the job of looking after them.

For two days the cubs would eat nothing. Joy tried again and again to persuade them to take tinned, diluted milk through a tube. On the third day she succeeded.

"Mm. Not bad," they seemed to think at the first taste. Then, "More, more, more."

She was kept busy now, cleaning the tube, and warming a mixture of diluted tinned milk, glucose, cod-liver oil, salt and bone-meal, and feeding the babies every two hours.

"We must give them names," she said.

"They're all girls," George reminded her. "This one is quite a bit bigger than the others."

"Right. We'll call her Big One."

"And this one's rather a jolly little thing."

"Yes. She is. We'll call her Jolly One."

"And the third one? She's smaller and weaker than

the others. I don't think she would have survived long in the wild."

"Elsa," said Joy. "We'll call her Elsa."

"Why Elsa?" asked George. Joy laughed.

"She reminds me of someone I used to know, whose name was Elsa," she replied.

In a very short time Big One, Jolly One and Elsa had settled happily into the Adamson's household. At night they were locked in a wooden shelter, but in the day time they were free to explore the house and the garden and the land outside. They grew rapidly and became stronger week by week. Like all young things they loved to play, but being young lions their play was especially energetic and boisterous. They did acrobatics in the trees. They tore banana leaves to shreds. They played ball games and had growling tugs of war with old car tyres. They played their own version of "king of the castle" and they liked pouncing games and dragging things about – in preparation for doing the same to animals they might kill for food in the future.

They had their own special guardian, an African boy called Nuru who watched them to see that they came to no harm, and who let them out of their shelter in the morning. This was usually their wildest time – the mad rush to freedom after the quiet night – the burst of energy and excitement at the prospect of a new day.

Once they gave a most disastrous welcome to two visitors who were sleeping in a tent. The cubs rushed in and out, bouncing on the amazed and horrified guests and carrying away shirts and slippers and cameras.

This adventure increased the cubs' pleasure in cushions and covers and books and belongings inside the house, so that soon, reluctantly, the Adamsons had to put the house itself out of bounds. Locking doors was useless. The cubs learned to undo them, so George put a high, bolted gate across the entrance to the veranda. It was made of strong wire netting, nailed to a wooden frame. To comfort the cubs he gave them some more toys to play with outside. He gave them a noisy wooden barrel to roll, and he hung a tyre from a tree. They could swing on this and jump at it and chew it. All the same they often rubbed their faces wistfully against the veranda gate asking plainly to be allowed in as before.

By the time the cubs were three months old, their teeth were getting big and they needed meat in their diet. A mother lion will chew meat up before offering it to her young ones, so Joy had to mince some every day. Elsa was still smaller and weaker than the others, so that she seldom managed to get her fair share of food. Because of this, Joy began to hold her on her lap at feeding time; and affection and trust grew strong between them. Elsa would often nestle up to her adopted mother, and caress her with her big, soft paws (claws held safely back) and suck Joy's thumb like a baby with a dummy.

Lion cubs in the wild do not leave their mother until they are two years old, for they have not learned to hunt and kill their own food before that. The Adamsons would be kept busy for a long time yet, and three lions growing bigger and stronger every day would be too difficult to manage. Something would have to be done about them. Reluctantly it was decided that only one could be kept. Arrangements were made for two of them to go to a zoo in the Netherlands at the age of five months. Which two should go? Which one should be kept a little longer? George asked the Africans who worked with him.

"Which lion shall we keep?"

"The smallest one."

"What do you say, Joy?"

"Oh, I hate parting with any of them, but you know which one I'll keep."

"Of course. Elsa."

So Big One and Jolly One went with Joy on an eleven-hour car journey to Nairobi airport. From there, they flew to the Netherlands, and sadly Joy returned alone. Elsa, meanwhile, was puzzled and upset. Where were her sisters? She looked everywhere for them. She looked around the house and in the bush. She called them again and again. She followed George a great deal and he let her into the house as of old. When he worked there in his office she settled down under his desk. When he retired for the night she slept on the bed with him.

Soon she became used to being an "only lion" and to take pleasure in the advantages that it brought to her. For example, when George and Joy went on safaris she was able to go with them, riding in the back of the Land Rover. She was able to share their camp life, to explore new areas of bush country and grasslands and rocks, and best of all, she was able to accompany them on an occasional holiday on the shores of the Indian Ocean. Puzzled and cautious at first, and wary of the roar of the waves, she soon grew brave enough to follow Joy and George into the sea when they swam. She played with them and splashed them in excitement, and derived as much pleasure from her games as a child on a seaside holiday would do. In fact, she was probably now becoming too human.

She regarded Joy and George as her parents. She understood what they meant when they said "No". She fitted well into their lives. She was polite and well-mannered. That she loved them there was no doubt, and her exuberant ways of showing it very often knocked them down. But she was growing bigger, heavier, stronger, older. Soon she would have to join her sisters in the zoo in the Netherlands, and this was something that Joy and George could not bear to think about. Elsa was so happy with them. She was used to almost complete freedom. A zoo, however good, would seem like a prison to her now. Yet she could not be returned to the wild. It is said that pet animals, put back among their own kind, were often attacked and killed because they carried a human smell and had lived an unnatural life.

. . . . . .

Time passed, and still Elsa stayed with the Adamsons. She was now more than two years old. She was almost grown up. She was used to all the animals in the area where she lived and the areas where she travelled and camped. She played with them or teased them or ran away from them or chased them, according to their kind and to her inclination – giraffes, elephants, antelopes, zebras, baboons, hyenas. In the day time Nuru always guarded her with a gun at his side. He sat beside her while she dozed in the sun. He followed her at a distance when she wandered into the bush. In the evenings Joy and George always took her for a walk. She followed them without any trouble, or came bounding back at their call, but now she was changing. She did not always obey their call. She sometimes went her own way and refused to return, and sometimes she was away for many hours.

One evening she would not come back after her walk. She sat down and refused to move. Darkness descended and the moon was very bright. Lions were calling in the distance. Elsa gazed into the bush, tense and trembling. Joy and George left her and returned later, calling,

"Elsa, Elsa, come back." She saw them. She heard them, but she could still hear lions too. Suddenly she stood up and stretched herself. She turned and took a few steps towards the lions.

"No, Elsa, no!" cried Joy. "You'll be killed." Elsa stopped. She looked towards her "parents". She looked back again towards the lions. Slowly, unwillingly, she followed Joy and George home.

It could not last. Elsa wandered away more often. Sometimes she was away all night. Sometimes she was away two or three days at a time. Then she would come home hungry and thirsty. The Adamsons had always provided her with food – raw meat, cut up ready to eat. Would she learn how to kill for herself – to hunt a buck or a zebra and pull it down and tear it apart? The land was dry now, but soon the rains would come and then water at least would be no problem. Sometimes Joy and George had time to follow her tracks and find out where she had been. More than once they found a lion's paw marks beside her own. She seemed to be meeting her own kind without any apparent danger to herself.

"It's worth trying," said George to Joy one day.

"What is?"

"Letting her free in the wild. She seems to get on all right with other animals – even with other lions. We would have to take her a long way from home so that she could not come back for food. Then hunger would force her to kill for herself."

It was an experiment that took a long time to come to its conclusion. George had some months of leave due to him, and instead of taking a proper holiday, he and Joy spent the time camping in another area, trying to teach Elsa to kill and hoping she would eventually find a mate and settle down with him. They drove away and left her for two or three days at a time. When they came back, she would often be waiting for them, miserable and hungry. Sometimes she would find her own way back to the camp and show quite plainly, that though she liked to wander, she really wanted to be with them. She would nestle up to Joy, caressing her with her big, soft paws, and sucking Joy's thumb in the old way. She was a wild lion and she loved the ways of the wild, but she was also partly human in her needs and habits. She belonged to two different worlds. Could she ever give up one and be truly happy in the other?

She was learning to kill, for when she returned to the camp now, it was sometimes obvious that her stomach was full. At times she joined other lions for a day or two, but she always came back as if rejecting them, or being rejected by them. Then one evening a lion roared from the distance. Obviously for Elsa it was a very special lion giving a very special call – an invitation perhaps, or a request. Elsa shook herself and left the camp. It seemed as if she had at last accepted the fact that she was a wild lioness. It seemed that a wild lion had accepted the fact too.

. . . . . .

So that chapter of the story ended happily, but a new, surprising chapter began. When it was clear that Elsa was not coming back to the camp, the Adamsons returned to their home. They felt very sad, for the great, gentle lion had been part of their lives for more than three years, and they missed her as much as ordinary parents would miss an only child.

Because George was senior game warden, he always had to travel a great deal; and sometimes Joy went with him on long safaris, sharing in his camp life and drawing and painting African tribesmen, animals and flowers. About once in three weeks they went to the part of the bush where Elsa now lived. When they arrived, George would fire into the air and they would set up camp for two or three days. Within a few hours, Elsa would arrive, knocking the Adamsons over in her delight at seeing them, putting her great paws on their shoulders and nuzzling her head against their faces in a great show of affection. Sometimes she would stay all night even though she knew her lion was waiting for her in the bushes, and even though he called for her in the darkness.

Elsa's pleasure at seeing Joy and George was always unmistakable, yet her enormous strength and power were held in check while she was with them; and when they left again, or sometimes before, she would return to her lion mate. Elsa herself had built a bridge between her two worlds.

Yet there was still more to follow. Later, Elsa gave birth to three cubs. She fed them and protected them and taught them the ways of the wild; and from time to time, she took them into the camp to visit her trusted human parents.

The information for this story was taken from Joy Adamson's book *Born Free* published by Collins.

More Iguanodons

In a museum in Belgium, there is a display of eleven iguanodon skeletons in standing position and twenty others arranged on the floor. This is the result of twenty-five years of work, supervised by a man called Louis Dollo.

The skeletons were found all in one place in the year 1878. They were buried in a coal mine three hundred metres below the ground, and were discovered while miners were digging a new passage. The men had actually dug through one skeleton without knowing it. As soon as they realised it, they reported the find, and the next three or four years were spent marking and mapping the position of the numerous bones, and then digging them out, cleaning and preserving and mounting them.

The strange thing was that there were bones lying in ordered arrangement at different levels of the earth, proving that long ago there must have been a great ravine down which the iguanodons had fallen. Some were killed by the fall, and others had probably starved to death before being buried by later piles of mud deposited upon them by flood waters.

Why had so many of the same species of dinosaur met their death in the same way, in the same pit? There are two main theories:

1 A herd of iguanodons had perhaps been disturbed and pursued by some even larger, fiercer dinosaurs, and in their flight, had fallen headlong into the pit.

2 As there were no skeletons of young iguanodons in the pit, it is possible that a group of old ones had gathered nearby to die, and had then been overtaken by sudden floods, and swept to destruction in the ravine.